Diving Equipment

Choice, maintenance and function

ISBN 978-1-909455-13-9 (Paperback)
ISBN 978-1-909455-14-6 (EPUB ebook)
ISBN 978-1-909455-15-3 (PDF ebook)

Cataloguing-In-Publication Data A catalogue record for this book can be obtained from the British Library.

Printed by Lightning Source.

Published 2016 by

Dived Up Publications
Oxford • United Kingdom
Email info@divedup.com
Web www.DivedUp.com

Diving Equipment

Choice, maintenance and function

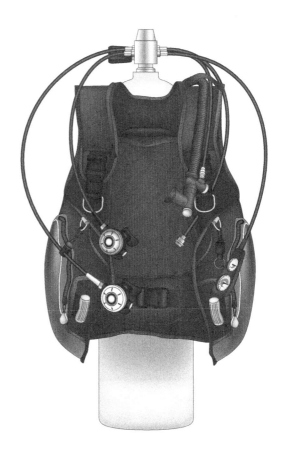

Jonas Arvidsson

DIVED UP

Table of Contents

About the author

Even being born and brought up by the sea, diving was not in my mind until I got tired of university, packed my backpack and bought a single ticket to Asia. After a few months wandering, I eventually ended up in the Philippines. Beer was cheap (it still is) and life was easy, but it became a bit monotonous after a while. Beside the bar was a diving centre and the activities looked interesting. I signed up for the next course and on the first dive I was hooked.

Diving soon became my full-time occupation. Continued education went quickly and I dived almost every day. Instructor jobs in Australia, the Philippines, Thailand, and after a while in Sweden. It was a massive conversion to dive in cold waters, but I quickly started to appreciate this special dive environment as well. I continued to move on, head of education at Professional Association of Diving Instructors (PADI) Sweden, dive centre owner, PADI Course Director, and translation of virtually all PADI training materials into Swedish.

Everything has its own time and with two children I decided to get a real job, so I bit the bullet and finished my interrupted studies. I managed to have a normal job too, but after 15 years in the formal school system as a teacher of biology and chemistry and later headmaster, and with offspring who are no longer children, the choice was easy to re-comply with my passion to share my knowledge of the sea.

Thanks!

This book would not have been possible without the knowledge that several curious and passionate divers contributed over the years. We are all indebted to these known and unknown pioneers who expanded human understanding of how we can adapt to experience the amazing underwater world. Many have succeeded in developing the technology; more have failed. We have learned with gratitude from all, none mentioned, none forgotten. But it was Émile Gagnan and Jacques-Yves Cousteau that started and inspired so many. So, a very special thank you to these two heroes from France.

Preface

Our equipment is a necessary part of diving, as we cannot truly experience the amazing underwater world without it. A mask provides an air space that our eyes need to be able to see clearly underwater. Our cylinders and regulators allow us to considerably extend our depth and time underwater.

Your entry-level training included aspects of physics and physiology. This dive theory was neither in-depth nor difficult to learn, it just taught you the knowledge you needed to become a safe diver. Your entry-level training also introduced you to the basic diving equipment that you needed to scuba dive. By lecture and practical experience you learned how each piece of equipment works and basic maintenance procedures to look after it. The training, however, was really not in enough depth to help you to make purchases and maintain your own dive kit. Knowledge of how different types of equipment work increases your ability to make the best choice when you buy your own equipment. Knowing how to take care for and maintain your equipment will make it last longer. It is a fairly big investment, so you probably want it to last for more than one season!

Despite this, you won't find many books on the subject of selecting and maintaining scuba equipment. A new diver turns to his dive instructor and looks at manufacturer sales materials. Catalogues and online reviews that parrot them give brief technical descriptions about how the equipment really works and how it should be used. The purpose of this book is to help educate you about the variations in equipment and thereby inform your choices. We hope that it will help you to get a better understanding of the aids that we have to increase our pleasure below the water's surface.

This book is based around a large number of illustrations, and the content is structured for self-study, but it can, of course, also be used as a tool for formal lessons during a course on diving equipment and for reference after the course.

This book aims to provide an international perspective on diving and diving equipment. While it is probably safe to assume that most recreational dives are done in tropical climes, this book discusses a wide spectrum of diving conditions. The book states both the metric and imperial measurements for most items, but note that neoprene thickness only uses metric. Legislation and rules in different parts of the world vary, so it is important to meet other divers locally to get an introduction to the conditions and rules where you dive. Air is used as a concept, but many of the discussions also apply to diving with other gas mixtures.

It would be impossible to cover every available piece of diving equipment in one affordable book. Fashions come and go. Good ideas and products fail to take hold and are eventually removed from sale. If something does not become popular it does not necessarily mean it was not a good idea. The reverse may also be true and time usually tells. For these reasons there are no brands or specific products mentioned by name in this book. Instead the most important, most common, tried and tested items of kit are covered. Your own view of what works and what is best will likely change as your diving develops, so re-read relevant sections later on and you may find a renewed perspective.

A description of special equipment for underwater photography and video is beyond the ambitions of this book. Instead, you should seek further information in any of the many excellent books written about these subjects. For example, *The Underwater Photographer* by Martin Edge (4th Ed., Focal Press: 2009).

Of course, you are not fully trained after reading just this book (or any other). Nor is it a substitute for formal certification. But it will help you on the way to becoming a better diver. Continue to develop your skills through experience, try out new equipment, read about scuba diving and look up specific questions online. Other scuba divers are an invaluable source of information. There is almost always someone who knows more than you about something, has been where you dream to go or has used the equipment you are curious about. After a day's diving when everyone is sitting around is a great time to ask your questions.

Introduction

Before starting to describe the features and functions of different pieces
of equipment, here are some general considerations for selecting it.

Camel diving safari, Dahab, Egypt.

Manufacturers' websites and brochures give a good overview of the products available on the market, but nothing compares to testing kit. You won't know if you feel comfortable with it until you try.

When you try to decide what diving equipment you should buy there are many factors to consider. Clouding your judgement will be a wide range of different brands and models, often with little to differentiate between them. You must sort out the confusion and learn to recognize the differences, in order to pick out the right kit for the diving you will be doing.

The first thing you must decide is what type of diving you will be doing. If you only intend to dive in warm tropical water you don't need a thick suit and you have no need of a freeze-protected regulator. However, for diving in colder water these items become very important. Fortunately, a large part of your scuba gear can be used for any type of diving. So, if you dive in varied conditions, you should buy equipment that will perform well in the most demanding environment you intend to dive in. Then only your thermal protection must be changed when diving in different water temperatures.

Once you've decided what type of diving you will do, you can look at the individual components of your scuba gear. The most important consideration is that the equipment must be safe. You won't really find any bad equipment on the market, at least not in serious dive shops, but there is some less reliable kit around.

It is important not to compromise on safety, just like when you buy a car. This is especially important if you buy used equipment from private advertisements. Properly maintained equipment can last a long time. Poorly maintained equipment, especially regulators, can become dangerous in a single season.

It is also important to have a complete set of equipment. If due to economic reasons you choose to delete some part of the equipment, you do this at the expense of you or your buddy's safety. If unable to buy everything at once then buy it in related stages (e.g. buy a full set of regulators, including an octopus) and rent what you have not yet purchased.

Since dive equipment, with the right care and maintenance, has a fairly long life expectancy it's a bad idea to start with 'beginners equipment' expecting to later trade up to better and better stuff. In the long run this will be more expensive than if you buy good equipment from the beginning.

However, in the beginning it can be difficult to know what suits you, so it can be a good idea to rent different types of regulators, suits and BCDs to see what you find most comfortable. Comfort is a very important factor when you choose your equipment. Your diving will be more relaxed and therefore safer with equipment that fits properly and you are comfortable with. This is why you should buy equipment that you get on well with and that fits you. This is especially important for mask, fins, suit and BCD. A wetsuit that is too tight on the surface may restrict your breathing at depth. A leaking mask, over-tight-fitting fins, a too big suit or a too small BCD can easily ruin a dive, or worse.

Servicing

Even the very best equipment will sooner or later need to be serviced. Cylinders and regulators will also need a regular service irrespective of how much or little they are used. When you buy your equipment you should ask if you can get this service where you live or dive. In most cases, this means that you go back to the dive shop where you bought the equipment. It is also important to check if they are authorized (by the manufacturer) to do a professional service on the brand you buy, as well as having the proper tools and spares. Think ahead—if you buy cheap equipment abroad on holiday you can't be sure that you even have a representative for the brand in your country.

All these considerations can be summarized in one simple point—you should buy your gear from a professional dive shop. There the trained staff will guide you to what is right for you and the diving you will do. Beyond professional level services, they can help give advice on how to maintain your equipment, so it works without any problems during your dives.

Regulator service engineers require approved training, service manuals, access to parts and the right tools.

Fully Equipped

Tropical or Warm Water

The warmer the water, the less need there is for protection against hypothermia. This means that you may not need any suit at all. It is much simpler to dive without a diving suit, buoyancy adjustments become easier and you do not need as much lead. However, it is important to realize that even a tropical climate can chill you since the water is still cooler than your body temperature. Diving from a boat it is often easier with full-foot fins and, if you travel a lot, consider equipment that is as light as possible.

1. Mask

Eyes must be surrounded by air to be able to focus. Your mask is therefore essential if you want to be able to experience all the beauty that is underwater. It is important that the mask fits your face, so that you can relax during your dives and not spend most of the time clearing water from it.

2. Snorkel

This may seem like an unnecessary part of the equipment for scuba diving, but a snorkel can be helpful on the surface. It is easier to breathe through the snorkel at surface swims or if you are waiting for a boat to come and pick you up.

3. Fins

By using our strong leg muscles, we move much easier than by swimming with our arms. Try a few different types of fins to find out what suits you and your diving best, we all have different pre-conditions in terms of strength and endurance.

4. Suit

Our body temperature is generally at least 10°C/18°F higher than the water we dive in. The cooler water draws heat from our body. The larger the difference between our body temperature and the water temperature the greater the rate of cooling is. If you only do a shallow dive per day in tropical climes, you may manage without a diving suit, but in most cases you will want to have some form of insulation against hypothermia. At higher latitudes you must have a good suit and it may be necessary to use a drysuit to be able to enjoy the experience.

5. Buoyancy Control Device (BCD)

The BCD gives you positive buoyancy on the surface and enables you to be neutral underwater. If you are diving with a drysuit, you normally use the suit for buoyancy control during the dive, but use the BCD to obtain positive buoyancy on the surface. You can also attach other equipment to a BCD, for example alternative air source and pressure gauge, to make you more streamlined underwater.

6. Cylinder

Without compressed air or other breathing gas there will be no scuba diving. Dive cylinders are available in aluminium or steel, different sizes and pressures adapted to local rules for pressure vessels. Normally this is not a part of the equipment that you take with you when you travel to foreign dive destinations. Airline restrictions on carrying compressed gas cylinders and the cost for the extra weight make them impractical for air travel.

7. Torch/flashlight

This is an obvious tool to take on night dives, but a good, small light on day dives can be used to shine into cavities and to bring out true colours at depth.

There is obviously no clear answer as to what a 'fully equipped' diver is. It depends on so many factors—where you plan to dive and what the goal of the dive is, for example. You will find that basic kit in most cases enables you to have enjoyable and safe dives.

Temperate or Cold Water

Diving in colder water places greater demands on your equipment. Regulators must be protected against freezing so that they do not freeflow due to icing. They must also be able to provide enough air for your breathing, drysuit and BCD. A drysuit and any layering will add buoyancy, so your weight must be adjusted so that you can maintain buoyancy control. The type of cylinder is also a consideration; heavy steel cylinders are a better choice than aluminium.

8. Knife/line cutter

In the early days of diving the knife was a weapon, a protection against all the devious creatures that lurked below the water surface. Today, we are better educated and consider the knife more of a tool to be used if caught in a fishing line or to examine something we would not want to touch directly with our fingers.

9. Regulator

Use approximately the same logic as for cars—there are no really bad products on the market and you get what you pay for. If you want a good regulator that can be used under different conditions in varying diving environments, you will pay more compared to a regulator which is adapted for easier diving in tropical waters. We can make it more complicated by comparing various tests and manufacturers' advertising; however, the most important thing is that you find a regulator that you feel comfortable with and that you can have serviced where you live.

10. Alternate air source

These are a few different options: most common is an extra second stage, but this does not help if you run out of air. An independent air source is better because it can help both you and your buddy in an emergency.

11. Instruments/dive computer

Technological development has given us many options to monitor our dives. Whatever we choose, we have to be able to keep an eye on depth, time and tank pressure. This can be done with everything from analogue instruments (watch, depth gauge and pressure gauge) to a dive computer that monitors all these parameters and tells us how long we can stay at the current depth with regard to dive profile and remaining air.

12. Weights

Most equipment configurations mean that you have positive buoyancy, at least at the end of dive. This must be compensated for with an amount of added weight. How much depends on a variety of factors, such as whether diving in salt or fresh water, the buoyancy of your suit and type of cylinder.

Importance of Tests

Comparing similar products from different manufacturers is second nature to humans. We look at price, quality, durability and an array of other factors. Impartial organizations and publications do independent testing. Naturally this is true for diving equipment. These tests can be presented in many ways, from simple overviews of what is on the market, to grading and giving opinions on their performance and whether or not they are worth their price. Manufacturers often refer to independent test results in their advertisements. When it comes to diving equipment, the regulator is the only piece of equipment for which the independent test is critical. For items like the mask, snorkel, fins, BCD etc., fit, comfort and personal considerations outweigh any results from independent tests.

When discussing performance, you often hear how 'easy breathing' a certain regulator is. Breathing resistance is easy to measure, but it is important to realize that you can do this in several ways. The most simple but hardly scientific way is to put the regulator in your mouth on the surface and breathe from it. This subjective method does not show much variation between modern regulators of different brands and models. More telling is their performance at depth during extreme conditions. If you are faced with a situation where you must swim against a strong current at 30 m/100 ft depth or if you need to help a stressed diver with your extra second stage at that same depth, you will realize what your regulator is capable of. Buying a high performance regulator is a bit like buying a car with anti-lock brakes (ABS) — you don't notice it until you need it.

What is CE Marking?

Conformité Européene (CE) is French for 'European Conformity'. CE marking is a common European standard whose purpose is to eliminate barriers to trade like national safety requirements and standards. A product approved in one of the member states can be sold freely in the whole area. Previously, manufacturers had to adapt products to suit the rules of each individual country, which took time, cost money, and limited the free exchange of goods.

A product may bear the CE mark and be sold in the member states if it meets specific requirements for the protection of consumer health and safety or the environment. Requirements vary between different groups of merchandise.

To meet the standards, a manufacturer must carry out a conformity assessment that shows that they and the product comply with European Union (EU) legislation. In addition to this, the manufacturer must also compile a technical description of the product, including a manual. The manufacturer must also issue an affirmation, which means signing a statement that the product conforms to the specifications from the EU. As a general rule, the manufacturer itself determines if the product meets the requirements.

For products that are considered particularly dangerous or where safety is very important, more stringent control is needed. This means that the manufacturer must turn to an independent test facility to establish that the standards have been met. Only an approved body situated within the EU/European Economic Area (EEA) can perform this control. As proof that the product is considered to meet the requirements, the testing facility issues a control certificate. This certificate is valid in all EU/EEA countries.

In the directives for personal protective equipment (PPE), equipment is divided into three different categories, each with a different set of requirements for the manufacturer and testing:

Category 1—The manufacturer can complete the risk analysis. This category includes simple PPE classes such as sunglasses and gardening gloves.

Category 2—A certificate from an independent testing facility is required. This group contains equipment that doesn't belong to category 1 or 3, like hearing protectors and protective helmets.

Category 3—In addition to the inspection certificate, the company must have a documented production control, for example, ISO 9000. This group includes equipment that can cause serious health hazards if it malfunctions, e.g. gloves which protect against heat or chemicals, and diving equipment.

The EU standards for diving equipment have been adopted as international standards, so wherever you buy your gear it should be CE approved. But always check before buying.

See *Chapter 5* 'Breathing Apparatus' for more information on standards, tests and comparisons between different regulators (page 136).

Preparation

Unpacking newly purchased scuba gear at a dive site is hardly good preparation. This should be done before you go diving to avoid hassles or errors. Practice putting the gear together a few times, putting it on and adjusting straps. Find the most comfortable way to place the different items. Think about how you intend to use the kit and check that everything will be easily accessible. More specific tips appear in individual chapters.

Care and Maintenance

You will not find many divers who consider their diving equipment consumables that should be used as long as they work and then be discarded. The majority of us want our investment to give us reliable service for many years. Each chapter explains what you can do to prolong the life expectancy of your equipment, and what you should not do or are not recommended to do.

Common for all diving equipment is that it should be carefully rinsed in fresh water after every dive and then be hung up to dry. Preferably, drying should not be done in direct sunlight and the equipment must be completely dry before you pack it away for storage. If you are careless with this, your equipment will soon become damaged by mildew or salt build-up. Even if you spend time with this basic care, your equipment will sooner or later show signs of normal wear and tear. This mainly depends on the number of dives you do, but also on ageing of the material. In order to give more specific advice, we must first consider the different pieces of equipment, so look out for tips in each chapter.

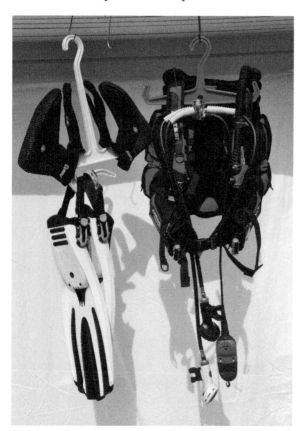

All diving equipment should be carefully rinsed in fresh water after every dive and then be hung up to dry. Preferably, drying should not be done in direct sunlight.

CHAPTER 2

Mask, Snorkel and Fins

With the right equipment, it is easier to relax underwater—you won't need to expend energy on a leaking mask or compensating for fins that are too small for you. Carefully selected, your mask, snorkel and fins can be used for diving, snorkelling and freediving.

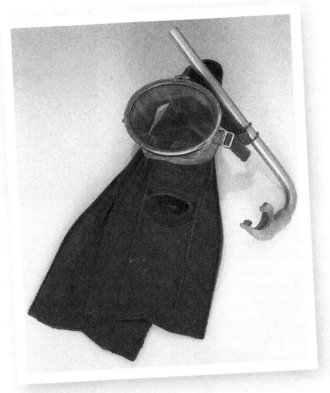

Snorkelling gear from the end of the 1950s.

Mask, snorkel and fins are the basic tools for our explorations underwater. They are not only used for scuba diving, but also for a relaxing swim on the surface, looking down into the water.

Snorkelling and freediving are activities that should not be underestimated. In some situations, using just basic equipment can be better than diving with a full scuba outfit. A shore dive with a reef just three metres deep, means no dragging of your tanks to the dive site. Scuba exhaust bubbles may scare off some fish; a whale shark will seldom come close to a diver but will frequently approach to within a few feet of a snorkeller. With a little practice, you can soon become proficient at getting a few metres down to take a closer look.

Humans have dived for a long time, but it was not until 1928 that we got what looks like a pair of swimming goggles. It was the American Guy Gilpatrick, author of *The Compleat Goggler* (1938), living on the French Riviera who sealed a pair of pilot goggles with putty. Gilpatrick inspired famous underwater explorers like Hans Hass, Jacques Cousteau and other legends to start skin diving.

Even if fin prototypes were introduced a few years earlier, it was Louis de Corlieu who first patented his design in 1933. However, it was Owen Churchill who made them popular among the general public, partly with the help of the swimmer Johnny Weismüller ('Me Tarzan, you Jane'). By 1954 he had sold 2 million pairs!

It was another Frenchman, Maxime Forjot, who took out a patent on both mask and snorkel, also in 1933. It took a long time to understand that the glass had to be in one plane to avoid double vision. This was solved with one piece of glass instead the two used in swimming goggles—and it got the appropriate name 'Cyclops'.

With functioning equipment, the big breakthrough soon came for skin diving. At this time, the activity was entirely focused on spear fishing or food collecting, an activity we debate today, but which was totally accepted at the time.

Mask

The early Cyclops has been replaced with the modern low volume mask. There is a trend towards 'frameless' masks, but the majority on the market have a soft silicone skirt and a rigid frame that keeps the tempered glass in place.

Cyclops

It is a little strange that such a fundamental thing as how to be able to see properly underwater was not actually solved until 1959, when the first single-lens mask that could be equalized appeared. This mask, with a flat lens and nose pockets, was preceded by a variety of different solutions, which all had their disadvantages. Cyclops was for long the standard for both divers and snorkellers. Formally it is known as an oval mask. The company U.S. Divers marketed an oval mask under the trade name Cyclops in the 1950s.

The name Cyclops comes from Greek mythology. Cyclops was a giant with only one eye in the middle of his forehead.

Modern low volume mask

It can be tricky to select a new mask because there is such a variety on offer, but this is probably the most important equipment-related choice you have as a scuba diver. The mask must fit your face and the diving you will be doing. An uncomfortable mask or one that leaks can ruin the best dive. So choose with care.

Neck strap
All masks have an adjustable neck strap for added comfort. Most are wider at the back to prevent slipping and to distribute pressure evenly.

Frame
A rigid frame keeps the lenses in the same plane. It must also be non-corrosive. Most frames are therefore made of some kind of plastic. Cheaper masks have nylon frames, but manufacturers use polycarbonate for better quality masks.

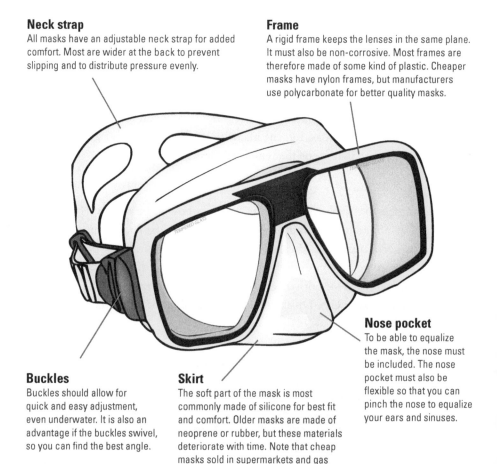

Buckles
Buckles should allow for quick and easy adjustment, even underwater. It is also an advantage if the buckles swivel, so you can find the best angle.

Skirt
The soft part of the mask is most commonly made of silicone for best fit and comfort. Older masks are made of neoprene or rubber, but these materials deteriorate with time. Note that cheap masks sold in supermarkets and gas stations may look like they are made of silicone but the material is a form of plastic. These are unsuitable for diving.

Nose pocket
To be able to equalize the mask, the nose must be included. The nose pocket must also be flexible so that you can pinch the nose to equalize your ears and sinuses.

Most silicone masks are transparent, but some are coloured black. The skirt should be soft and flexible, and preferably have a double seal around the face to prevent water from entering. The exception is under your nose, so that water may drain more easily during mask clearing. Even if the skirt feels soft and flexible, you must try to find a mask that fits you. The best way to check the fit is to place the mask on your face and inhale through your nose. If the mask stays in place without you or the strap holding it, it fits.

Tempered glass

Tempered glass resists scratching and breakage better than normal window glass. If broken (in the dive bag or by a dropped weight belt on the boat deck), the tempered glass will crumble into many small pieces that stick together. This is less dangerous than shattering into a few larger sharper pieces. Check that 'Tempered Glass' is etched in the glass. Lenses are available in a few different forms:

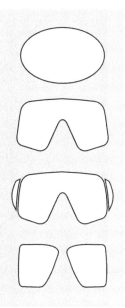

Oval—the classic Cyclops. Large volume but gives a less 'trapped' feeling.

Single lens—combines Cyclops and two-piece mask.

Side Windows—gives a wider field of vision.

Two-pane—the most common type. Low volume and wide field of view. Shape of the lenses varies.

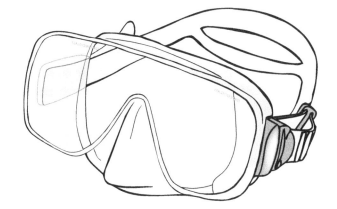

Frameless mask

Frameless masks are becoming popular. The silicone skirt is attached directly to the single lens. This gives a good field of vision, low volume, low profile and a lighter mask. The swivelled mask buckles are moulded to the silicone skirt.

Diving with a visual impairment

If you have impaired vision there are a number of different ways to correct this for scuba diving:

- Small problems may be corrected by the normal refraction of light in water.
- If you are short-sighted, this is often a minor problem because you will be able to read your instrument displays. There are usually also many interesting things to see close to you during a dive.
- You can also dive with contact lenses; just make sure you close your eyes if you need to clear the mask as there is a risk of losing them.
- If you have other challenges with vision, there are a number of different solutions...

Replacement prescription lens

Most manufacturers have 'optical' masks. These have separate glass and you buy ground lenses in 0.5 dioptre increments. The replacement is easy to make and the cost is about the same as for a pair of good quality spectacles. Ground lenses are only available for the most common corrections, so this won't help everyone.

Prescription lens bonded to the mask

Most optometrists can bond prescription lenses to the inside of your favourite mask if you are near-sighted and only want to have reading glasses in the mask or if you have a more complicated visual impairment. The price is often a little higher, but then you also get a mask that is perfect for you. This may be the only option if you can't find ground lenses for your favourite mask or if you have an impairment that can't be corrected with ready-made solutions.

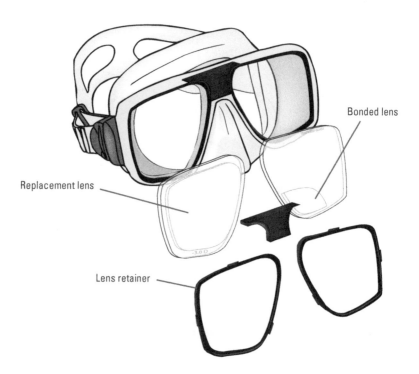

Bonded lens

Replacement lens

Lens retainer

Lens retainers

Masks utilise various solutions to attach lenses. So if you must change to prescription, examine exactly how the lenses are attached before removing them. The most common method is plastic retaining rings, which are held in place with small trims in a few different places. It is important that these do not break off when you remove the rings, and that they are pressed firmly into place once you have made the change.

Purge mask

This type of mask is not especially common today. The compromise here is a large volume and often a wide field of view. Such a mask is more difficult to clear because of the large volume, but this is facilitated by the presence of a valve in the bottom of the nose pocket.

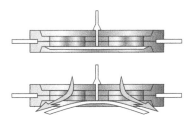

This type of check valve (a one-way directional valve) is the same sort found in most modern snorkels. A thin silicone membrane seals against a plastic frame. Pressure is higher on the outside of the membrane, but when you exhale through your nose, the pressure is higher inside the mask compared to the outside and hence the water in the mask is forced out.

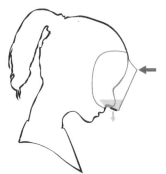

Mask clearing — standard mask
This is most likely very familiar to you. When clearing a mask without a check valve, you look upwards, hold the top of the mask rim and exhale through the nose. The water in the mask is pressed out from the lowest part of the mask, which is just behind your nose.

Mask clearing — purge mask
When clearing a mask with a check valve, you look downwards so the valve is the lowest part, hold the top of the mask rim and exhale through the nose. The water in the mask is forced out through the check valve.

Special masks

Camera mask

This is a standard diving mask with a built-in digital camera for still images and video. The great benefit is that you have your hands free when you dive or snorkel and that the camera faces whatever you look at.

There are compromises: First, does the mask fit your face? Second, accept that the images will not be the same quality as a camera in a waterproof housing with separate flash/light. But as an easy way to capture memories from your dives it works well.

Development is fast in the digital world, not least when it comes to cameras. If you are interested in buying a camera mask, check out the market and compare performance—both for camera masks, digital underwater cameras, action cameras (e.g. GoPro) and standard cameras in waterproof housings.

Full-face mask

For diving in very cold or contaminated water, this is an excellent device. The mask covers the entire face and the big single lens gives a much larger field of view compared to a conventional mask. You do not breathe through the regulator via a mouthpiece, instead there is an internal mask that covers both mouth and nose—so you can breathe through both your mouth and nose in a full-face mask.

This also provides the advantage that it is possible to connect a communication system so that you can talk with your buddy or people on the surface. Most full-face masks have excess pressure inside the mask to prevent the lens fogging-up.

As you probably realize, there are a lot of challenges when diving in a full-face mask. You should properly consider if this is something for you, for example:

- What do you do if you run out of air, or for any reason cannot breathe from your primary air source?
- Does the full-face mask work with your first stage regulator or do you need to buy a new one? (Some use a lower intermediate pressure than most diving regulators).
- How do you manage surface swims?
- Does the full-face mask fit your dive suit hood?
- Do you want to have ambient pressure or over pressure in the mask?

- The internal volume is large, which gives increased buoyancy at the head. How will you manage this?

As you can see, a full-face mask requires special training. If you have come to an educated decision to dive with one and manage all the challenges, it can be a very good tool for demanding diving conditions.

Heads up display (HUD) mask

This is a recent development in diving masks: a modern low volume mask combined with a dive computer, with the display inside the mask. This means that you have all of your important data directly accessible without having to look at your wrist or console. HUD-masks are still quite unusual, but development is fast.

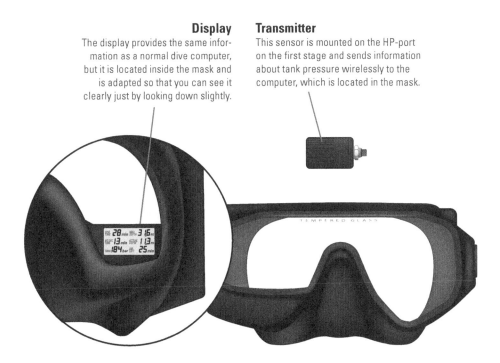

Display
The display provides the same information as a normal dive computer, but it is located inside the mask and is adapted so that you can see it clearly just by looking down slightly.

Transmitter
This sensor is mounted on the HP-port on the first stage and sends information about tank pressure wirelessly to the computer, which is located in the mask.

Accessories

There are not many accessories for a standard dive mask. The most common is a neoprene strap, which more easily slips over hair or a hood, holds the mask in place better and distributes pressure evenly so it is more comfortable too. Most also have an attractive design—for the dive centre, a brand or dive destination.

There are two different types of neoprene mask straps. The most common just slips over the original strap. The other type completely replaces the original strap. The adjustment is normally either Velcro or a buckle.

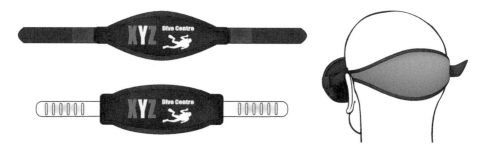

Fogging must be avoided if we want to enjoy our dives. The problem is caused by the air inside the mask being warmer than the water on the outside—your body warms it up. Warm air can hold more moisture than cold air, so when the warm air comes into contact with the cold lens, moisture condenses into water droplets. What we are doing when we spit in the mask or use an anti-fogging solution, is adding a wetting agent that reduces the surface tension of the water and thus the ability to form drops. The condensed water instead collects in the mask.

Saliva is, of course, easy to use because we always have it with us, but some divers prefer not to spit in their masks. An anti-fogging product in a convenient container solves this problem, but soap, shampoo, washing powder or alcohol work just as well. It is important to remember that the anti-fog solution, whichever we choose to use, should be applied to dry lenses otherwise a part of the effect is lost. Coat the inside of the lens with it and rinse to remove the excess. Then you can enjoy a clear view during the entire dive.

Bottled anti-fog product.   Always clean a new mask before using it for the first time.

However, even bottled anti-fog agents will not work unless the mask has been cleaned before first use. Most manufacturers put a protective coating on to prevent degradation during shipping and while on display. Any residues from the manufacturing process may also still be present. They are easily removed with toothpaste and toothbrush. Take special care to clean the inside of the mask lens, otherwise it will fog up during your dives.

Snorkel

A snorkel has some obvious advantages when snorkelling or freediving, allowing you to breathe without lifting your head out of the water. When scuba diving, a snorkel lets you save air and energy during surface swims.

A snorkel is basically just a bent tube with a mouthpiece, but we can hardly find any piece of equipment that has undergone so much 'development' in modern times. Designers have really worked their brains to come up with more or less functional valves to prevent water from entering the snorkel and to aid clearing. It is only natural to see a desire to develop more sophisticated tools for our pleasure, but now we seem to be back to more traditional models.

The snorkel is now much more than a bent tube. However, be aware of elaborate devices to keep water out. It is easy to clear water that may come in from a snorkel, so these devices are hardly essential.

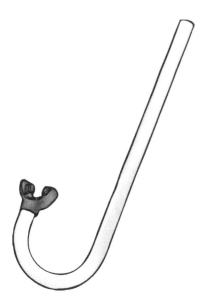

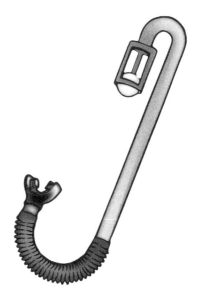

Bent tube

The first snorkels were made of aluminium with a mouthpiece in rubber. The tube was narrower than modern snorkels, so breathing resistance was greater. The deep bend also made it difficult to clear water.

Ping-pong snorkel

This type of snorkel was common in the 1950s and 1960s. The idea was that the device at the top of the snorkel tube, a ping-pong type ball in a basket, would keep the water out. Most often it did, but it also sometimes prevented air from entering. The corrugated bend made it difficult to clear all the water and it increased breathing resistance.

Modern snorkel

It is worth taking your time when choosing a snorkel. This is one of the items of your scuba gear that has multiple uses—when scuba diving it has its role on the surface and between dives you can use your mask, fins and snorkel to watch life below the water surface from a different perspective. For some divers, and especially in technical diving, snorkels do not have the same importance; on the contrary, they might be an obstacle. However, technical dive planning is so different that they have taken account of this.

1. Mouthpiece

Most modern snorkels have a silicone mouthpiece for comfort. A good option is a swivelling mouthpiece which enables you to find the best angle too. There is hardly anything more annoying during snorkelling than a snorkel that drags in your mouth. With a modern snorkel it is usually possible to find a comfortable position. Instead of a swivelled part at the mouthpiece, many snorkels are made of soft silicone in the lower third of the tube. This makes them flexible and they hang down when you don't have them in your mouth. Some divers prefer this when scuba diving, since it is more out of the way than a normal snorkel.

2. Purge valve

(see page 31).

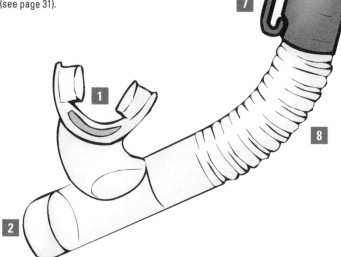

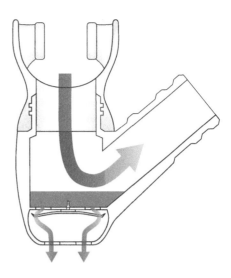

3. Splash guard

Some modern snorkels have a splash
guard at the top — with no moving
parts that can be caught.

4. Tube

The tubes of early snorkels were made
of aluminium, but almost all snorkels are
now made of a semi-rigid plastic. The
plastic gives manufacturers lots of possibilities in using colour in their designs,
so you can colour co-ordinate your kit.
The upper part of the tube usually has a
contrasting colour or is reflective to make
it easier to spot you on the surface.

5. Form

The first snorkels had a deep U-shape. Now
they are shaped to give less drag, be easier
to clear and give less breathing resistance.

6. Size

Modern snorkels are shorter and wider than
the first snorkels. This gives less breathing
resistance and dead space. A normal size
is 40 cm/16 in long and 2 cm/¾ in diameter.
A shorter snorkel is hardly practical for an
adult and a larger bore gives less breathing
resistance, but is difficult to clear.

7. Snorkel keeper

It is important that the snorkel stays attached
to the mask strap, but it should also be
easy to remove. There are many types of
snorkel keepers, but most manufacturers
include some kind of quick-release.

8. Flexible part

The soft silicone section swivels at both the
top and bottom attachment points, which
makes it easy to adjust the mouthpiece to
a comfortable position. It also means you
can move it out of the way whilst diving.

Purge valve

Most modern snorkels have a purge valve to
facilitate clearing. At the bottom is a check valve
that releases water with the help of gravity or
your exhalation. This makes it easier, requiring
less effort to clear the water from the tube. It is
important that the soft silicone membrane seals
against the ring, otherwise it will leak. So, rinse
this part carefully to avoid salt deposits. It is also
obvious that this part is sensitive to sand and
debris that can prevent the seal. Snorkels for
freediving do not usually have a valve — making
them as small and streamlined as possible.

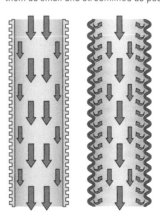

It is important that the flexible part of the snorkel
is smooth inside, with no corrugations which can
trap water and increase breathing resistance.

Fins

This is the part of our diving equipment that is closest to the adaptations which have evolved in swimming aquatic animals. Fish and whales swim with their caudal (tail) fins and we try to imitate this. Anyone who has compared using arms and legs for swimming underwater realizes what an advantage the strong leg muscles have for propulsion over the weaker arm muscles.

Churchill's duck feet

Even if there were predecessors, this was the first mass-produced fin. They started selling in 1940 and they quickly became popular with skin divers. When diving apparatus became available after the Second World War, new models on the same concept were developed. Surfers use primarily this type of fin today.

Force Fin

Taking inspiration from those early fins, the appearance of 'Force Fins' is quite different. Many wreck divers prefer these to the more common adjustable fins, for their power, simplicity and because they are well-suited to frog-kicking and finning backwards.

Jetfin

Jetfin was the first adjustable fin that was widely available. It was invented in 1964 by Beuchat in France, and is still being produced now. Jetfins are entirely made of rubber and heavy in comparison with modern fins. This can be a problem when diving in tropical climes with a thin dive suit, but when diving in a drysuit many divers prefer heavy fins in order to balance the buoyancy the suit gives around the legs.

Modern fins

There are two main types of fins: full foot fins; and adjustable fins. Full foot fins are best suited to snorkelling, freediving and scuba diving in warmer water from a boat, while adjustable fins are best suited for diving with boots or with a drysuit. So, before you buy fins you must consider what they are to be used for — it is possible that you will come to the conclusion that it is best to buy more than one pair of fins for the diving you will be doing.

Try a few different types of fin to feel what suits you and your diving best — we all have different predispositions in terms of strength and endurance!

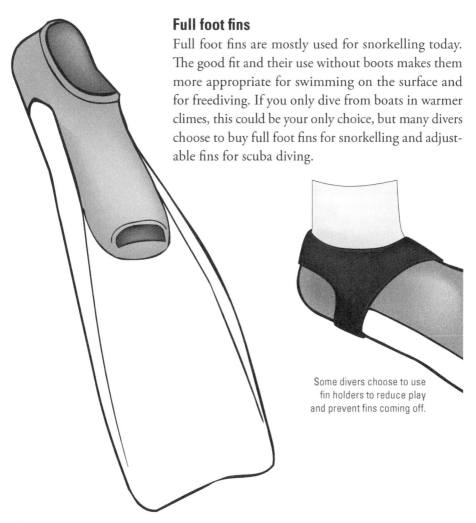

Full foot fins

Full foot fins are mostly used for snorkelling today. The good fit and their use without boots makes them more appropriate for swimming on the surface and for freediving. If you only dive from boats in warmer climes, this could be your only choice, but many divers choose to buy full foot fins for snorkelling and adjustable fins for scuba diving.

Some divers choose to use fin holders to reduce play and prevent fins coming off.

Fit

Full-foot fins must be correctly fitted, just like shoes — narrow fins are uncomfortable and if they are too large you lose efficiency. They are normally manufactured in two-size bands, such as 40/41, 42/43, etc. The foot pocket is made of soft, flexible rubber to facilitate donning and doffing and it is flexible enough to cover two shoe sizes.

Straps and buckles

On adjustable fins you need straps and buckles. Normally the fins have a broad strap with a quick release buckle for easy adjustment and removal. The buckle should swivel, so you can position the strap for best comfort and to avoid it slipping. A tab on top of the centre of the strap facilitates donning.
An accessory for most adjustable fins is a spring strap. This facilitates both donning and doffing because you do not need to adjust the length. Fixed, *non*-quick release spring straps are practically indestructible.

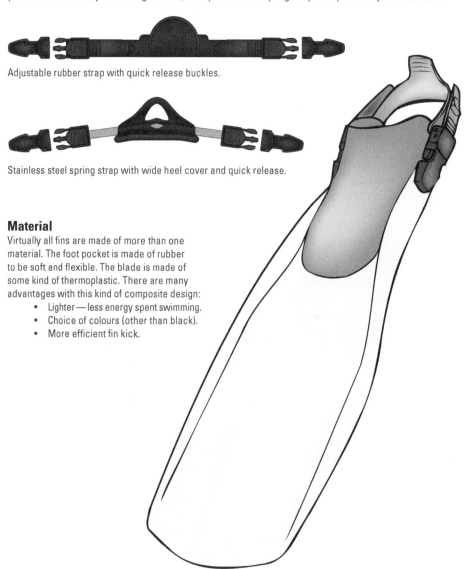

Adjustable rubber strap with quick release buckles.

Stainless steel spring strap with wide heel cover and quick release.

Material

Virtually all fins are made of more than one material. The foot pocket is made of rubber to be soft and flexible. The blade is made of some kind of thermoplastic. There are many advantages with this kind of composite design:

- Lighter—less energy spent swimming.
- Choice of colours (other than black).
- More efficient fin kick.

Adjustable fins

Adjustable fins come in a range of sizes from XS to XXL but vary by manufacturer and model. The fins must be tested with the boots or the drysuit you will dive with. It is important that your feet fit in the pocket, but there should not be too much free space. The strap gives scope for some adjustment, but it is still important that you buy the right size. For drysuit diving it is usually better to have a looser rather than a tighter fit so fins are easier to get on and take off.

Shape

The design should allow for efficient propulsion underwater. More modern forms of the blade have replaced the traditional 'paddle'. Manufacturers try to construct a blade which will channel water *backwards* as you swim — not just *up and down* with your kicks. On modern fins, blades have some form of rib system. Some fins also have vents in the blade to facilitate the upward kick — our leg muscles are not as strong in that direction.

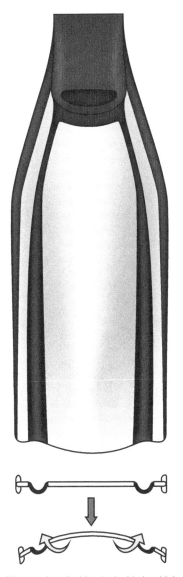

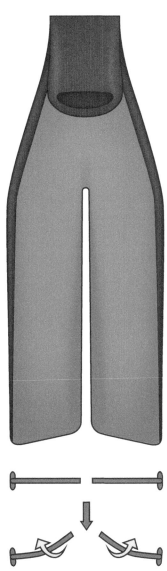

Ribs — strips of rubber in the blade which facilitate channelling, are common. They increase propulsion efficiency and provide better stability in both upward and downward kicks.

A 'split fin' has a divided blade. This gives good channelling of water backwards. Many divers find this type of fin easier and less tiring to swim with, but you need to kick at a slightly higher frequency, which not all feel comfortable with.

Type of fin

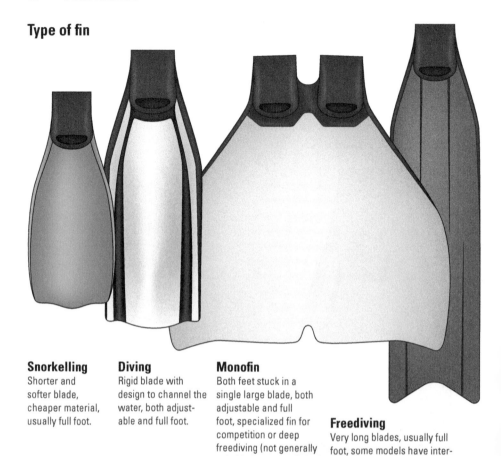

Snorkelling
Shorter and softer blade, cheaper material, usually full foot.

Diving
Rigid blade with design to channel the water, both adjustable and full foot.

Monofin
Both feet stuck in a single large blade, both adjustable and full foot, specialized fin for competition or deep freediving (not generally suitable for scuba diving).

Freediving
Very long blades, usually full foot, some models have interchangeable blades in different materials and length (not generally suitable for scuba diving).

The difference between snorkelling and freediving is often defined as being that snorkelling takes place for the most part on or around the surface (shallow), whereas freediving means diving below the surface, going deeper and holding the breath for much longer.

Choosing fins

The most important consideration when you choose fins is comfort. The differences between divers regarding size, strength, way of diving and dive location make it difficult to give general recommendations on which fins are best. It is better to try them out. Have this in mind:

- If you only dive from a boat in tropical waters, you are probably best off with a pair of full foot fins.
- If you dive in varied conditions, you should buy a pair of adjustable fins
- A larger and stronger diver should choose bigger and stiffer fins. A smaller diver should choose softer and smaller fins.
- Split fins — these are considered by many to be less tiring, but you must use a higher kick frequency when you swim with them.

Despite the fact that mask, snorkel and fins are the simplest items of dive kit, it is well worth the effort to carefully select them. With the right choice you can relax underwater, since you won't be irritated by a leaking mask or fins that are too small. Your mask, snorkel and fins could also be used for snorkelling and freediving—activities scuba divers should spend more time doing. Without scuba kit, you get more freedom exploring underwater, and with a little practice you will soon get down to 10 metres/33 feet or more without too much effort.

Care and Maintenance

These are often the first items of diving equipment that a new diver buys and their simple design leads many people to think that they are indestructible. The regulator, BCD and other expensive parts of diving equipment get full attention, while the mask, snorkel and fins are just thrown into the dive bag.

The problems that can occur are usually related to straps, buckles and connections. Many dives have been cancelled due to a mask or fin strap being broken while donning them. Inspect your straps regularly and change them at the first sign of damage or wear. It is also a good idea to have an extra set in your 'save-a-dive' kit (see page 173).

Today most masks are made of transparent silicone. This is a more expensive material than the traditional black rubber, but it lasts much longer. Rubber will sooner or later degrade by ozone and ultraviolet rays. However, it is important to consider how you store your silicone mask. Most come with a protective container. While the first impression is that the tempered glass needs to be protected, in reality it is the silicone skirt that is most prone to misuse and failure. Improper storage of the mask can lead to the skirt being weakened and even damaged. As the damage advances, it becomes more difficult to maintain the seal against your face. Keeping it in a protective case also helps to keep the skirt from being discoloured. A wetsuit can cause the silicone to be discoloured. This is also a consideration when you buy a snorkel—the snorkel keeper should be made of a material that doesn't discolour the silicone (plastic rather than neoprene rubber).

Problems with the snorkel are almost exclusively connected to the snorkel keeper. This small device has seen a lot of development and can consist of anything from a simple rubber band to advanced designs with a quick release buckle—check that it is not broken. If dirt or sand gets into the seal of a purge valve, the snorkel will leak. A build-up of salt from improperly cleaning your equipment can also cause it to leak. Normally it is enough to rinse the snorkel with fresh water to make it seal again.

Most modern fins have a quick-release buckle to ease putting on and removal. The buckles are often the weakest point on the fins. Both the part connected to the strap and the part that sits on the fin itself can break. Sometimes it is lost when the fins are taken off. If you have this type of fin, you should carry spares in your 'save-a-dive' kit.

CHAPTER 3

Thermal Protection

As all diving takes place in water that is a lower temperature than the body, you will sooner or later become cooler. There are a variety of ways to protect your body from this, depending on water temperature and the type of diving you are doing.

It can get quite chilly in the Red Sea in winter.
A 5 mm full wetsuit with hood is recommended.

Whenever we dive, even if it is in the warmest tropical seas, water temperature will be lower than body temperature. This means that we will lose heat. As you will remember from your entry-level course, water also conducts heat away from your body much better than air. This means that wherever we dive we must protect ourselves from getting cold. This was a big problem in the early days of diving. Commercial divers with helmets had fairly good drysuits that covered them up entirely except for their hands. But the material in these suits was too stiff to be used for swimming. The first drysuits for scuba divers were primitive and had no valves.

It was not until the early 1950s that neoprene foam was invented, and it was not long before wetsuits where made of this new material. Divers soon discovered that they did not need a drysuit to keep warm underwater; the passive insulation from the wetsuit was enough in most waters. The use of drysuits declined with the evolution of wetsuits, but for colder waters wetsuits did not provide enough insulation to be comfortable. Drysuit development continued and in the 1960s the first model with a neck seal, inflator valve, exhaust valve and airtight zipper came onto the market. The neck seal and the valves were new inventions and the zipper was a product of the NASA space programme. Now there are many different types and models of suits on the market, and this chapter explains the features and benefits of the most common ones.

Protection for Whom?

A dive suit is not only a protection against cooling; it also works as a mechanical protection against sharp objects, jellyfish, etc. It is important to note that the reverse does not apply: just because you are protected from the organisms that live in the sea does not mean that they are protected from you. Correct buoyancy and control of your body are better strategies to save both your suit and marine life.

More than One Suit?

Most pieces of our equipment can be used regardless of the specific environment, e.g. masks work equally well in warm tropical water and colder climes. This applies in large measure to everything, except the diving suit. There isn't really a compromise that can be used in all circumstances — we must choose a suit for the water temperature.

If you live at higher latitudes and dive under varying conditions, it is not usually possible to use just one suit for everything. It is often necessary to have both a drysuit for home waters and a thin wetsuit when travelling to tropical destinations. The wider your interest for the underwater world becomes, the more different diving suits you will need.

Drysuit is more adaptable

It may seem paradoxical, but the type of diving suit that has the maximum temperature range is a drysuit because the only real task it has is to keep you dry. The insulation can be adjusted with more or less under-clothing. So, select a diving suit with care — being cold during a dive is not fun! But with the right thermal protection you can dive comfortably in most conditions, even under ice.

Suit choice summary

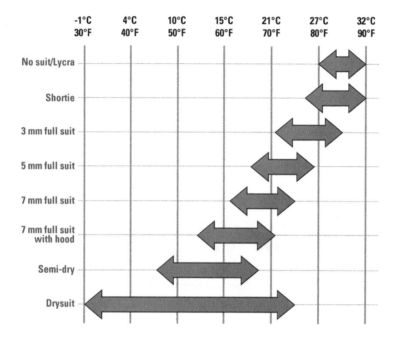

A **Lycra** suit is an elastic suit that is basically a swimming suit that covers part of (i.e. a rash vest), or the whole body. This gives hardly any protection against cooling, it is just a physical barrier against the sun and jellyfish stings. It can also be used under a wetsuit for easier donning and possibly reducing water circulation.

Shorties are suits with short legs and short or no sleeves. They protect the torso to some extent from cooling. A shortie works well for low-intensity diving in tropical climes, but if you are going on a dive trip for a few days and make three or four dives per day you may become uncomfortable with so little thermal protection. If you only intend to make one dive per day in tropical areas, you may not need a diving suit. But it is good to wear a t-shirt to avoid abrasions from your BCD.

A **full wetsuit** reduces water circulation in the suit, especially if it is of a good design and it fits you well. In cooler conditions, it can be supplemented with a hood as we lose a lot of heat from the head and neck if we do not protect these body parts. They are made in many styles and different thickness in different parts — e.g. legs and arms with 3 or 4 mm neoprene for increased mobility. It is impractical to use thicker than 7 mm material, so that is the only choice for colder water. Fixed hoods reduce water circulation in the suit as well as heat loss at the head and neck, but most suits have a separate one. Some models of thick wetsuits have a **two-piece** design — a jacket worn over a pair of long johns. This way you get double insulation over the torso.

A **semi-dry** suit is usually made of 7 mm neoprene with cuffs at the ankles and wrists, and a waterproof zipper. The hood can be fixed or separate. The aim is to minimise water circulation in the diving suit.

As indicated by the graphic on page 40, a **drysuit** has the widest temperature range — especially a membrane suit, because the only real task this has is to keep you dry. The insulation is determined by the amount and type of clothes worn underneath. Another advantage of a drysuit is that you are dry when you remove the suit, which means that you do not risk cooling further after a dive.

Wind chill

It is not only water temperature and the type of diving that you have to take into account. The weather on the surface also plays an important role. If it is warm and sunny, you quickly recover heat after a chilly dive — if it is cold and windy cooling can continue long afterwards. If you dive from an open boat, the apparent wind can also cool you down on the way home.

Calm	-1°C 30°F	4°C 40°F	10°C 50°F	15°C 60°F	21°C 70°F	27°C 80°F	32°C 90°F	Calm
3 m/s 7 mph	-4°C 25°F	1°C 34°F	9°C 48°F	14°C 57°F	21°C 70°F	27°C 80°F	32°C 90°F	11 km/h 6 knots
6 m/s 13 mph	-7°C 20°F	-0,5°C 31°F	7°C 45°F	13,5°C 56°F	21°C 70°F	27°C 80°F	32°C 90°F	22 km/h 12 knots
9 m/s 20 mph	-8°C 18°F	-1,5°C 29°F	6°C 43°F	13°C 55°F	21°C 70°F	27°C 80°F	32°C 90°F	32 km/h 18 knots
12 m/s 27 mph	-9°C 16°F	-2°C 28°F	6°C 43°F	12,5°C 54,5°F	20,5°C 69°F	27°C 80°F	32°C 90°F	43 km/h 23 knots
15 m/s 34 mph	-9,5°C 15°F	-3°C 27°F	5,5°C 42°F	12,5°C 54,5°F	20°C 68°F	27°C 80°F	32°C 90°F	54 km/h 29 knots
18 m/s 40 mph	-10,5°C 13°F	-3,5°C 26°F	5°C 41°F	12°C 54°F	20°C 68°F	27°C 80°F	32°C 90°F	65 km/h 35 knots
21 m/s 47 mph	-11°C 12°F	-4°C 25°F	4,5°C 40°F	11,5°C 53°F	20°C 68°F	27°C 80°F	32°C 90°F	76 km/h 41 knots

This wind chill table should only be seen as a general guide. There are many ways to calculate the wind chill factor, and it is important to realize that the table is based on dry skin. However, we can see that if the air temperature is above 20°C/68°F there is no problem, but under 10°C/50°F the wind is a factor you have to take into account — not only actual wind but also wind created on an moving open boat.

Wetsuits

The idea with a wetsuit is that a small amount of water seeps into the suit. This is quickly heated by the body and becomes a part of the insulation layer. If this water circulates, you will use a lot of energy to heat it up, so it is important that the wetsuit fits well and that you are moving in a way that reduces water circulation.

■ The water you dive in

■ Wetsuit

□ Water in the suit

□ Body

◄ Heat loss

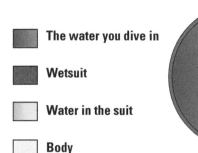

The water you dive in

Water temperature can differ greatly between the surface and your greatest depth. Generally temperatures decrease at a uniform rate. At higher latitudes there is often a thermocline in the summer. A thermocline separates warmer water from colder water. In this band the temperature decreases rapidly—it can differ by as much as 15°C/28°F between the top of the band and the bottom of it. The presence of a thermocline could cause significant temperature differences even as shallow as 25 m/80 ft. Thermoclines are also often found in deeper lakes. In the tropics thermoclines are not commonly experienced by divers, there is usually little difference between the surface and 30 m/100 ft.

Compression

A wetsuit insulates you from the surrounding water, so its effectiveness depends on how thick it is. The insulation is given by gas bubbles in the material. Because the wetsuit compresses as depth increases it therefore gives less insulation as it does so. At 15 m/50 ft a suit can have lost as much as two thirds of its insulating ability.

Water in the suit

The body heats a small amount of water quickly, even if it may feel a little chilly when you jump in the water. If this water remains in the wetsuit it becomes a part of the insulating layer, but if there is a constant influx the body must heat up the new water. A wetsuit that fits well and a scuba diver who moves deliberately uses less energy (and air) compared with a diver with an ill-fitting wetsuit who makes sweeping or erratic moves.

Body

Our body only works in a very narrow temperature range around 37°C/ 98.6°F. You will not find that many dive sites where the water holds that temperature, which means that when we dive, we will lose heat. The body's reaction is to create more heat through increased metabolism, a process that requires oxygen. This means that it is not only uncomfortable to be cooled underwater, you also use more air.

Heat loss

Heat loss, both real and perceived, depends on many factors:
1. More energy is used with an ill-fitting suit because of greater water circulation.
2. Thickness of the wetsuit, therefore the amount of insulation.
3. Ambient water temperature, especially at the depth where you spend the most time.
4. Air temperature — this determines if you feel warm before the dive and how quickly you recover after the dive.
5. Dive depth because the effective insulation depends on the ambient pressure — the thickness decreases with increased depth.

The arrows in the graphic on page 42 give you a general idea.

As the name implies, a diver will be wet in this suit. However, this doesn't matter as long as the water that enters the suit stays in it. If the suit fits snugly and you move carefully, the amount of water that enters will be limited. This water will soon be warmed and then become a part of the insulating layer. This, together with the insulating properties of the neoprene foam, helps prevent the body cooling. If the suit is too big or doesn't fit snugly, the body will be cooled quicker. For this reason, some manufacturers offer custom-made suits for those who have a body that doesn't conform to standard sizes.

Wet suit materials

Neoprene foam has been further developed since its invention in the early 1950s. Its insulating ability has increased and it is softer and more flexible. The first wetsuits did not have any lining on the inside or the outside. This made them difficult to get into and out of. Most suits are now lined on both sides and some even have an inner plush lining to help to reduce water circulation.

To further increase durability, many manufacturers add reinforcement at the knees, elbows and shoulders — the areas which experience the most wear. A suit designed with slightly bent knees will also encounter less wear, since this is the most common position in the water.

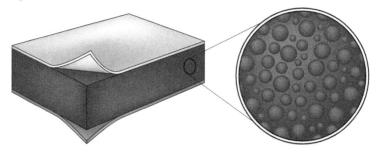

Neoprene is a form of synthetic rubber that has good chemical stability and which retains its flexibility in a wide temperature range. Application is wide-ranging, but for diving we are most interested in the foamed neoprene that is used in wetsuits and some drysuits. During the manufacturing process, nitrogen gas is added which creates small bubbles that do not come into contact with each other (as opposed to what happens with a sponge). This gives a waterproof, buoyant material with good insulating properties. To increase the strength a synthetic fabric is laminated to one or both sides; the latter is most common for wetsuits for scuba diving.

For higher quality suits, different types of neoprene are used for various parts of the suit to get the optimal balance between strength and mobility. Different types of lining can also be used to give a durable and stylish exterior and an interior with limited water circulation.

Gas bubbles in neoprene act according to Boyle's Law—they are compressed with increased pressure. So the thickness of neoprene and thus its ability to insulate decreases with increased depth. Since (in temperate regions at least) water temperature usually decreases with depth it would be helpful if it was the other way round, but we can't change the laws of physics. The material used will be the manufacturer's compromise between 100% neoprene rubber with its ability to withstand compression, and neoprene-butyl with its greater capacity to stretch and flex without tearing cells walls.

Chemicals that degrade neoprene are all acids, acetone, iodine, all types of grease and oil, urine and all liquids containing chlorine.

Joins

It is hardly practical to cast a wetsuit in one piece, so manufacturers must join the parts in some way. Most common is to start by gluing panels together followed by stitching them from the outside. In some cases, the seam is taped on the inside to make it even stronger. Better wetsuits and drysuits are glued and stitched on both sides, since this give a much stronger join. Some also have taped seams—reducing the risk of irritation to the skin.

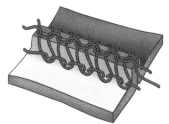

Overlock

This is the simplest and cheapest way of joining neoprene. Pieces are added on top of each other and sewn together. This gives a raised edge on one side of the suit (usually inside) and the seam allows some water flow. Overlock is rarely used for diving wetsuits and can only be used for neoprene up to 3 mm in thickness.

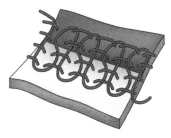

Flatlock

This provides a smooth seam that allows some water flow. It is rarely used in diving suits thicker than 3 mm. It does not reduce flexibility of the suit and it is flat on the inside.

Adding a nylon band over the neoprene and then flatlock stitching it gives a strong and flat seam, but it allows some water circulation. This is standard on thinner diving suits, but it reduces flexibility of the suit—a problem that can be minimized by not using it at all places on the suit or by using a band of stretchable material.

Blind stitch

The neoprene pieces are first glued together and then stitched—but the needle does not penetrate all the way through the material. This gives a strong, waterproof seam that is used for virtually all modern wetsuits for diving from 5 mm thick and upwards. A band can be bonded to the inside for increased strength, but usually only on particularly vulnerable places because it reduces flexibility.

Higher quality thicker wetsuits are stitched on both sides. This gives a strong bond that still provides full flexibility of the material.

Zippers

To ease dressing and undressing, suits are made with one or more zippers. Zip placement varies with the imagination of the designer, but the most common positions are vertically on the front or back, or horizontally across the shoulders. Some suits also have zippers at the ankles and wrists. These are most common on wetsuits made for diving in warmer waters since they normally increase water circulation in the suit. However, it's quite common to find neoprene padding under the zippers to make a better seal and increase comfort by keeping the zip away from the skin.

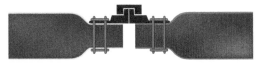

Basic zipper

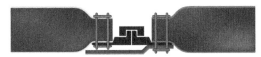

Zipper with seal on the inside

Models

Shortie

A short suit mainly used for diving in the tropics, for wind-surfing, water-skiing and other surface activities. Shorties only provides limited protection against cooling and some abrasion protection. These suits are most often made of 3 mm neoprene. Not all shorties are alike. Shorties designed for surface activities often use a neoprene grade that is not designed for the compression of even a shallow dive.

'Over shorties' are designed to be worn over a full diving suit to increase insulation. The hood can be fixed, but models without hood can also be used as a standard shortie. Over shorties are usually made in 5 mm neoprene.

Full wetsuit (overalls)

This is in principle the same diving suit as a shortie, but with long arms and legs. A full suit can be made with or without a hood and the zipper can be placed on the back or front. Closures at wrists and ankles can be made with zippers to facilitate dressing and undressing. Unlined neoprene cuff seals reduce water circulation. Made of 3 to 7 mm thick neoprene.

Two-piece suit

Normally made with long trousers (long johns or farmer Johns) and a jacket with long sleeves. The hood can be separate or attached to the jacket. Two-piece suits are mainly used for diving in colder waters, and made of 5 to 7 mm thick neoprene. The advantage with this design is that you can use the long johns and jacket separately, or together to provide double insulation — giving you some flexibility. The disadvantage is that a lot of neoprene is used in the production of the suit. This not only makes the suit more expensive, but also more buoyant. You might think that the double layer of neoprene over your torso will give better insulation, but a two-piece suit will normally hamper you by more water circulation than a one-piece design.

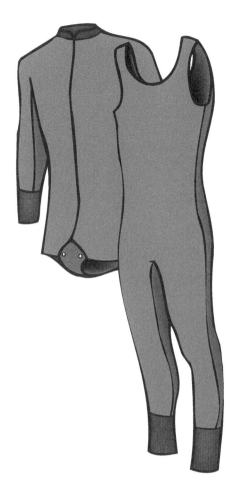

The jacket can be made with or without a fixed hood and different thicknesses can be used at different locations to optimize movement and insulation. Closures at wrists and ankles can be made with zippers to facilitate dressing and undressing. Unlined neoprene cuff seals reduce water circulation. Some companies offer a long sleeve shortie instead of a jacket.

Semi-dry suit

The most common wet suit design for use in colder waters. A semi-dry suit is a one-piece design with seals at the neck, wrists and ankles and sometimes with an attached hood. Some models also have a waterproof zipper. This keeps water circulation to a minimum. Semi-dry suits are normally made of 5 to 7 mm thick neoprene, and you can find different solutions for the seals, similar to drysuits (see page 56).

Higher quality suits use different types of neoprene at different places to optimize movement and insulation. Can be supplemented with a vest for increased insulation. Many models also have a double layer across the back for increased insulation and cushioning.

Accessories

Hood

Since we lose a lot of heat from the head and neck, it's a good idea to invest in a hood. For scuba diving in colder water a hood is a must. As you have seen, many wetsuits made for colder water have a hood attached to the suit, but some divers prefer to use a hood even when diving in warmer waters.

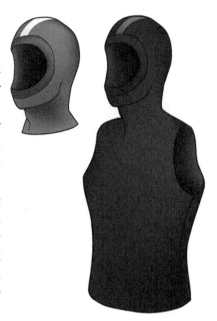

Separate hoods normally cover only the head and neck, but some models are connected to a vest or wide collar. This reduces water circulation and gives increased insulation (and buoyancy) over your chest. Be aware that a separate hood always means greater water circulation in the diving suit than a fixed hood.

Hooded vest

A hood attached to a vest not only provides insulation for the head and neck, but also for the torso. This solution can be a good option to extend the range of a full wetsuit instead of buying different diving suits. See also the information on 'Over shorties' on page 46, which have a similar function.

Gloves

In colder water, it is often necessary to wear gloves to avoid cooling. As a rough guide to thicknesses: 3 mm below 15°C/59°F, 5 mm below 12°C/53°F and 7 mm mitts below 8°C/46°F—but it depends on the individual. For diving in tropical waters, you can have thin gloves with no insulation. They only act as a mechanical protection. Gloves made of neoprene are always a compromise between insulation and manual dexterity—thicker material gives better insulation but less dexterity. They are available in 1.5 to 7 mm neoprene. Those made for diving in colder water often have a longer collar with a Velcro closure around the wrist to reduce water circulation. Other features include lining (to make them easier to put on and take off), semi-dry seals and zips.

To increase effectiveness when diving in cold waters, you can use mittens or lobster gloves (three fingers). The advantages are a thicker material, fingers warming each other and the water having a smaller area to draw heat from. The disadvantage is reduced dexterity.

Thin gloves

Many dive centres in tropical areas do not allow their guests to wear protective gloves. The reason for this is that you are likely to be more careful and more aware of where you are in relation to the reef. They are usually allowed on wreck dives.

Gloves should not be used as a protection against the reef. The best way to protect coral reefs against deterioration from divers is, of course, to practice good buoyancy and keep an eye on where your fins are!

Thick gloves

Thickness is a balance between insulation and mobility. Thick gloves are usually made of 5 mm neoprene. When diving in cold water your fingers are an important consideration — freezing fingers can be a safety hazard with adversely affected dexterity.

Lobster gloves

By keeping your fingers together you lose less heat to the water. Just make sure you can manage your equipment with these gloves — they should not be a safety problem. It is a good idea to practice in shallow water before you make a full dive to make sure that you can manage your inflator and all your equipment, buckles and releases. Usually 5 or 7 mm thick. Also called mittens or just 'mitts'.

Boots

Neoprene boots are a necessary part of the wetsuit for most divers. The majority will dive with adjustable fins for which you *must* have boots. For most types of diving it is a good idea to have some kind of protection on your feet anyway. Naturally, we have the advantage of extra insulation, but also the extra mechanical protection boots give against fin chafing, as well as when you walk on land or deck to and from the dive site. At one time divers used neoprene socks, but they have been superseded by boots with a hard, ribbed sole and a zipper to facilitate donning and doffing. Due to the hard sole, it is important to choose fins with a pair of boots on and not only select them based on the size of your feet.

There are not many types to choose from:

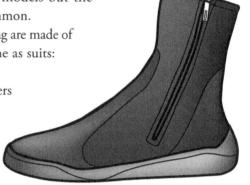

1. Height — there are some low models but the height in the image is most common.
2. Thickness — most boots for diving are made of the same thicknesses of neoprene as suits: 3, 5 and 7 mm.
3. Zipper — most boots have zippers to facilitate donning and doffing, but some models do not, reducing both price and water circulation.

Socks

If you prefer to dive with full foot fins you can buy soft neoprene wetsuit socks in the same thicknesses as boots. They insulate against the cold, but also help avoid abrasions from fins. The fins must be tested with the socks — you cannot normally use the same full foot fins for diving both with and without these socks.

Neoprene allergy

Some people are allergic to neoprene and this can develop over a period of use. The problem shows itself as urticaria (hives) in sensitive areas such as the neck, armpits and groin. The cause is residues of the chemicals used in the manufacture of the neoprene. Research is on-going to reduce or get rid of these chemicals, so if you have this problem, one solution could be to check out which neoprene supplier the various wetsuit manufacturers use. Cleaning the inside of the suit with mild detergent may remove chemical residues. Showering yourself after diving (again, using mild soap) may help. You can also try wearing a rash vest. If the problem persists you should see your doctor and he or she may suggest you are tested for allergies. Another way is to dive in a drysuit (see the next section) or suit alternatives for warmer water that do not use neoprene, but a material more similar to thick fleece.

Drysuits

For all those who dive outside the tropics, it is natural to dress according to prevailing weather conditions and season. In winter we dress in thicker clothes and in the summer we wear lighter garments. So it is easy to understand that we must do the same when we dive — both on land but in particular according to the greatest depth we intend to dive to.

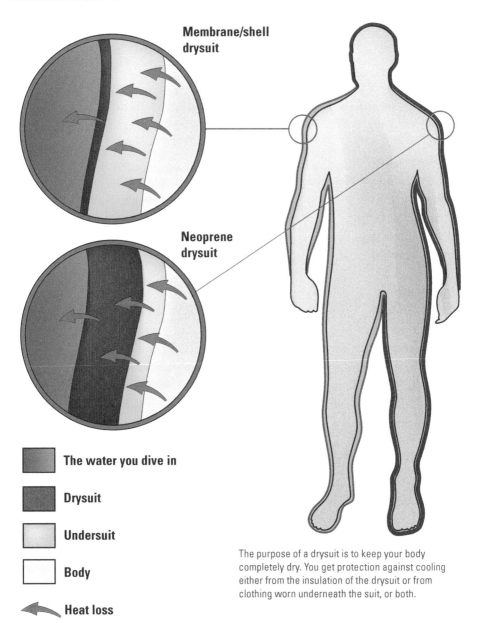

Membrane/shell drysuit

Neoprene drysuit

The water you dive in

Drysuit

Undersuit

Body

Heat loss

The purpose of a drysuit is to keep your body completely dry. You get protection against cooling either from the insulation of the drysuit or from clothing worn underneath the suit, or both.

Many dives are made on tropical coral reefs—it is warm, easy and beautiful, but diving in cooler waters should not be underestimated. There are many areas outside the tropics with equally good diving and as interesting wildlife as the coral reef. However, the diving requires a little more consideration—not least when it comes to the diving suit.

The water you dive in

The water temperature can differ a lot between the surface and your greatest depth. At higher latitudes in the summer there is often a thermocline where the temperature decreases rapidly—it can differ by 15°C/28°F between the surface and 25 m/80 ft! But in the tropics there is little difference between the surface and 30 m/100 ft.

The two types of drysuit

A drysuit keeps the surrounding water out. Most modern drysuits are made of neoprene foam or some kind of coated fabric.

Membrane/shell

The only task this suit has is to keep the water out—there is no built-in insulation or buoyancy—you decide on the amount of insulation by wearing more or less clothes. The undersuit is most commonly a jumpsuit with a wind proof exterior filled with compressible fibres (like a sleeping bag). A shell suit provides neither insulation nor buoyancy if it punctures during a dive.

Neoprene

The efficiency of a neoprene suit depends on its thickness and the exact type of neoprene used, but is also affected by depth. Neoprene drysuits are made of the same material as wetsuits so have both built-in buoyancy and insulation (even if they puncture). With a neoprene drysuit, you don't always need thick undergarments, often it is sufficiently warm with a plain tracksuit. The insulation is given by gas bubbles in the neoprene, but as these will be compressed with increasing depth so the suit will insulate less, which is a clear disadvantage, especially on deep dives.

Undergarments

A traditional neoprene drysuit provides insulation, but you may need to combine it with undergarments depending on the water temperature. Thinner neoprene drysuits, however, necessitate more clothes to provide sufficient insulation. Also note that the insulating ability of traditional neoprene decreases with increased depth, meaning that you must wear warmer undersuits for deeper diving.

When diving with a membrane/shell suit, the water temperature and your preferences determine the amount of insulation you need. The suit will not be compressed with increased depth. This means that a shell suit might be the most flexible solution if conditions vary a lot where you dive.

Body

Our body only works in a very narrow temperature range around 37°C/ 98.6°F. You will not find that many dive sites where the water holds that temperature, which means that when we dive, we will lose heat. As already noted, the body's reaction is to create more heat through increased metabolism, a process that requires oxygen. This means that it is not only uncomfortable to be cooled underwater, you also use more air.

Heat loss

We assume that the drysuit is not leaking. If it does, it will become a very expensive semi-dry wetsuit. A leaking shell suit can become dangerous because it does not have any buoyancy or insulation. Heat loss, both real and perceived, depends on many factors:

1. Amount of insulation.
2. The ambient water temperature, especially at the depth you spend the most time.
3. The temperature on land—this determines if you feel warm before a dive and how quickly you recover after the dive.
4. (Neoprene suits only) Dive depth because the effective insulation depends on the actual pressure—the thickness decreases with increased depth.

The arrows in the illustration (on page 51) give a general idea.

Advantages over a wetsuit

Even if a wetsuit satisfies your needs for most diving situations, we can identify some obvious drawbacks. The most important ones are:

1. Insulation will be reduced with depth. Since normally the water temperature reduces with depth, we have an impossible equation to solve.
2. The wetsuit will maybe give you sufficient insulation during the dive, but the heat loss before and after could be considerable. If you change at the dive centre and go by small boat to the dive site, you will be cooled on the way. On the way back, the moisture on and in the suit will further cool you down. In addition, not many divers will enjoy donning a cold and clammy wetsuit for their second dive, or taking a suit off outside when it is cold and windy.

With a drysuit you can avoid all these problems, but a drysuit is more expensive and requires more care and maintenance than a wetsuit. However, most divers at higher latitudes consider it worth the price, since the advantages are so clear.

Neoprene drysuits

This is the same material used for wetsuits, normally 5–7 mm thick. The difference is that the manufacturer ensures the panel seams are waterproof. Good quality neoprene suits are always sewn on both sides (with blind stitch—see page 45).

The advantage of a neoprene suit is that it gives good insulation and you only need special undergarments when you dive in extremely cold water. These suits also have built-in buoyancy, which is an important safety consideration in an emergency. Due to the flexibility of the material, neoprene suits tend to be a better fit than shell suits. This also makes it easier to move since they create less drag in the water.

In order to reduce the problems of decreased insulation and buoyancy with increased depth, some manufacturers make neoprene drysuits in thinner material or in crushed neoprene.

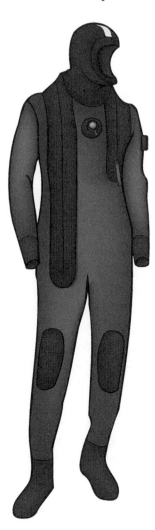

Compressed/thin neoprene

Often incorrectly considered to be the same thing as crushed neoprene, compressed neoprene is in fact regular neoprene foam (which is compressed during normal manufacturing). Normally made of 2–4 mm thickness material. This reduces the variation in insulation and buoyancy, and gives a more flexible suit compared with both thick neoprene and crushed neoprene. The structure of the material, however, is the same as in standard neoprene, although possibly with smaller gas bubbles.

Crushed neoprene

The suit is made in normal neoprene foam and then it is subjected to a patented process that crushes and flattens the gas bubbles in the material. The result is a drysuit with constant buoyancy and insulation (since the bubbles do not compress further at depth). The trade-off is less flexibility—but they are tough and durable suits.

Membrane/shell suits

These suits are made of a coated fabric and their only purpose is to create a waterproof shield around your body. To dive comfortably in a shell suit you need some kind of undergarment to create sufficient insulation. This is a versatile suit, since you can adjust your undergarments to suit the water temperature.

Urethane-coated nylon

The most common material used is urethane-coated nylon with seals in latex. This makes for a relatively cheap suit and the seams are both sewn and heat-sealed.

Trilaminate

Membrane trilaminate drysuits are becoming increasingly common, as the material is both strong and lightweight. As the name suggests they consist of three layers, ballistic nylon fabric with a layer of butyl rubber in the middle. Some manufacturers also have models with a breathable middle layer for diving in warmer water.

Trilaminate: Drysuits intended for warmer waters can be made of a breathable material. Different types of fabrics can also be used on specific parts of the suit—for example, greater abrasion resistance at the knees or stretchier over the shoulders.

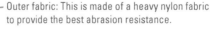

Outer fabric: This is made of a heavy nylon fabric to provide the best abrasion resistance.

Middle layer: The middle layer is usually made of butyl rubber, which is stable and flexible for the actual temperature range. Thinner drysuits made for warmer waters can be made of a breathable Gore-Tex type middle layer.

Inner fabric: The inner fabric is normally polyester to provide some flexibility.

Vulcanised rubber

Vulcanised rubber drysuits are more flexible than urethane-coated nylon ones, but they are heavier and bulkier. Rubber suits are only generally used by commercial divers who need the extra protection and durability.

The disadvantage of shell suits is that the material is totally inflexible. So these suits must fit quite loosely so that they do not restrict the diver's movements. Unfortunately, the result is that the suit gets quite wrinkled, and increases water drag. Another disadvantage is that a shell suit doesn't have any insulation or buoyancy, so they are not as warm as neoprene suits (at least at shallower depth) and you have to rely totally on your BCD for buoyancy in an emergency. If you get water in a shell suit you also lose all insulation as your undergarments will get wet. A large leak will lead to quick cooling and a small incident can become a serious one.

Seals

These are normally made of neoprene on neoprene suits and latex on membrane/ shell suits. Some divers prefer latex, since this gives a somewhat more flexible and better seal. The disadvantage with latex is that the material is more fragile and can easily rip while dressing if the diver is not careful. Furthermore, a latex seal doesn't give any insulation around the neck and wrists, so they become places where you lose a lot of heat.

Neoprene two-piece wrist seal
Made of two layers of neoprene with lining on one side only. When dressing, the unlined sides are located against each other. Then, before you put gloves on, the inner piece is folded back so that the unlined side seals against your wrist. The unlined side of the upper piece will then also seal against the skin.

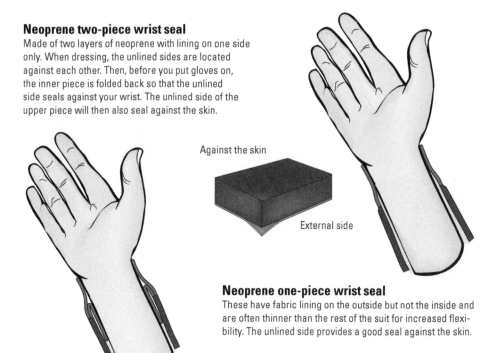

Against the skin

External side

Neoprene one-piece wrist seal
These have fabric lining on the outside but not the inside and are often thinner than the rest of the suit for increased flexibility. The unlined side provides a good seal against the skin.

A relatively recent development is silicone seals. Silicone is a softer material than latex and reduces problems with allergic reactions for those who are hypersensitive to chemicals in latex or neoprene. However, silicone cannot be glued or welded to the suit, so these seals must be used in conjunction with some form of ring system. For more information about different wrist seals see about dry gloves under 'Gloves/ mitts' on page 65.

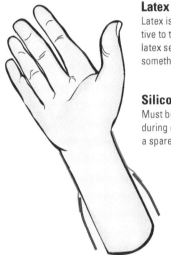

Latex

Latex is flexible and provides a good seal against the skin, but is sensitive to tearing and ozone and air pollution causes it to deteriorate. If a latex seal rips it is quite complicated to replace it, and it is definitely not something you do at a dive site.

Silicone

Must be used with a ring system. If a seal is ripped during dressing, it is easy to replace provided you carry a spare — see 'Gloves/mitts' on page 65.

Neoprene neck seal

Most neoprene neck seals are only lined on one side. When dressing, the skin slides against the fabric lining. Once the suit is on, you fold the neck down inside itself so that the unlined side seals against the skin. It is also common to see latex neck seals on neoprene drysuits since latex is more comfortable and dressing is easier.

Latex

Most shell suits and some neoprene drysuits have latex neck seals. Latex is flexible and provides a good seal against the skin, but is susceptible to tearing and ozone and air pollution deteriorates it. If a latex seal rips it is quite complicated to replace it, and it is definitely not something you do at a dive site.

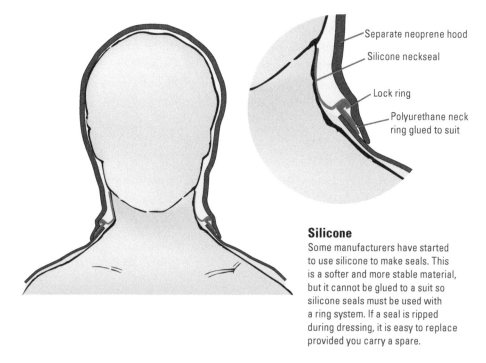

- Separate neoprene hood
- Silicone neckseal
- Lock ring
- Polyurethane neck ring glued to suit

Silicone

Some manufacturers have started to use silicone to make seals. This is a softer and more stable material, but it cannot be glued to a suit so silicone seals must be used with a ring system. If a seal is ripped during dressing, it is easy to replace provided you carry a spare.

Zipper

The zipper on a drysuit must be totally waterproof. As mentioned earlier, the gas and waterproof zipper was a product of the NASA space programme. Before this invention, divers had to rely on more or less imaginative solutions for entering the suit (like a roll-closure at the waist). The zipper is the most vulnerable part of the drysuit. It requires some extra care and maintenance to give you perfect service—see 'Zipper' on page 70.

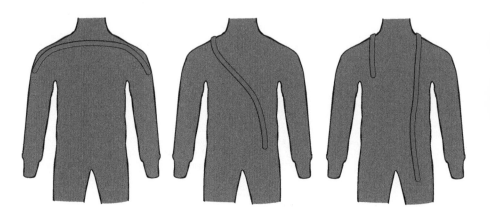

Over the shoulders
Comfortable location, but requires assistance to close and open. Short zipper.

Across the torso front
Convenient location, can be closed and opened without help.

Around the neck
Unusual, but convenient location, can be closed and opened without help. Long zipper.

The most common zip location is horizontally across the shoulders. This doesn't restrain movability, but the disadvantage is that you can't close or open it yourself. The main alternative is diagonally across the front of the torso, which can be opened without your buddy's assistance. The location is a compromise between easy dressing, length (as short as possible) and minimizing restriction during diving.

Metal dry zipper

This has moulded-in metal parts which lock into each other. The seal is over and under these hooks, which means that the sealing surface is larger compared with a drysuit zipper made of plastic.

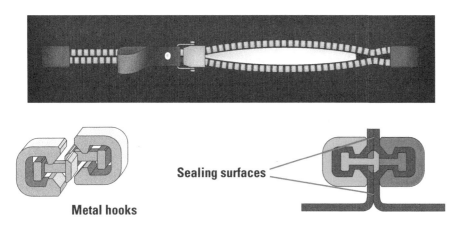

Plastic dry zipper

This is a high standard zipper with teeth on both the outside and inside. The teeth press rubber edges against each other to give a completely sealed closure.

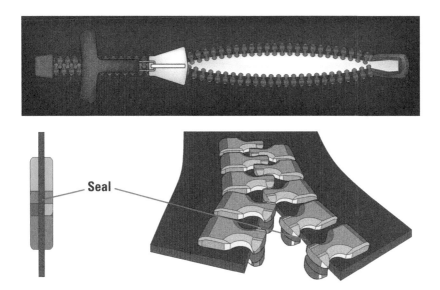

Valves

To use a drysuit for diving you must be able to adjust the amount of air in the suit. Some divers prefer to use their BCD to control buoyancy, like they do with a wetsuit, but they still have to add some air to their drysuit during the descent to prevent 'suit squeeze'. However, it is more common to dive with an empty BCD and use the drysuit for buoyancy control. In that case the BCD is only used to create positive buoyancy at the surface. This way the drysuit acts in exactly the same manner as the BCD, so when you descend you must add a little air to the suit, and vent some during the ascent. The drysuit inflator is normally placed in the middle of the chest and connected to the first stage of the regulator, just like the inflator on the BCD. Most exhaust valves are placed on the upper left arm (as air naturally migrates to the highest point). There are manual and automatic valves (most common). With an automatic valve, you adjust the release pressure and it will open when the pressure inside the suit exceeds this. Closing it at maximum depth helps to avoid losing small amounts of gas during the dive. Older drysuits may have a 'cuff dump' on the right forearm, but this is not as good since it restricts movement of the arm while diving, to avoid accidental exhaust when the cuff might be the highest point.

A separate cylinder with argon gas is sometimes used for filling the drysuit, especially when helium is used in the breathing mix. Argon has significantly better insulating properties than helium and better than air, but the cost per dive increases.

Automatic exhaust valve
An automatic valve on the left upper arm is now the most common solution.

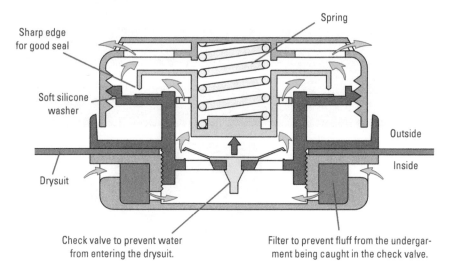

Spring

Sharp edge for good seal

Soft silicone washer

Outside

Inside

Drysuit

Check valve to prevent water from entering the drysuit.

Filter to prevent fluff from the undergarment being caught in the check valve.

Most exhaust valves on modern drysuits are semi-automatic. This means that a spring-loaded valve releases air from the suit when the pressure becomes greater than a set value. Turning the outer ring varies the spring tension, so it is possible to adjust the release pressure to your preference.

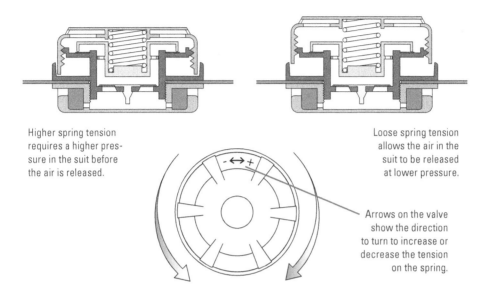

Higher spring tension requires a higher pressure in the suit before the air is released.

Loose spring tension allows the air in the suit to be released at lower pressure.

Arrows on the valve show the direction to turn to increase or decrease the tension on the spring.

Inflator

The inflation valve is a simple mechanical design where a spring-loaded plunger closes and opens the valve.

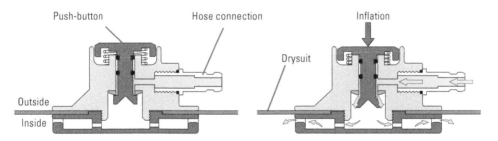

The hose that comes with the suit is installed to a low-pressure port on the first stage. The connection to the inflation valve can be of two different types. One option is the standard inflation hose, the same international connector used in nearly all BCDs — see 'Low-pressure hose connection' on page 79. The other is a CEJN-connector.

CEJN-connector

The standard BCD connector provides a limited airflow, so some manufacturers instead use (and you can also sometimes choose to have) the CEJN-connector, which gives a greater airflow. Another advantage of this connector is that you don't need to pull back the collar to connect the hose and it is easier to remove it—good for thick gloves or stiff/cold fingers.

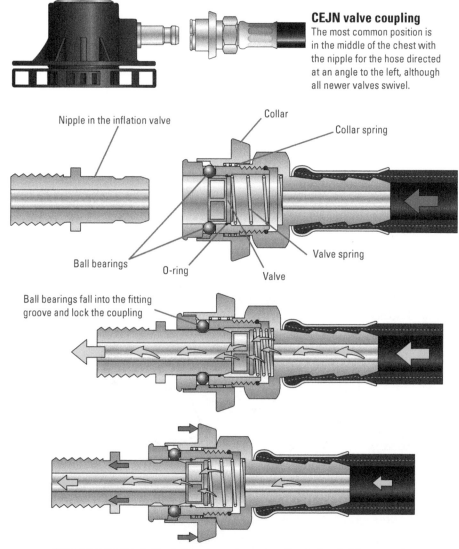

CEJN valve coupling
The most common position is in the middle of the chest with the nipple for the hose directed at an angle to the left, although all newer valves swivel.

Nipple in the inflation valve

Collar

Collar spring

Ball bearings

O-ring

Valve

Valve spring

Ball bearings fall into the fitting groove and lock the coupling

When the collar is pulled back, the valve spring presses the nipple out of the connector. When the valve is pushed forward, it seals against the O-ring in the connector.

When the connector is pressed against the nipple it locks without the need to pull back the collar because it is locked in this position with ball bearings. The front part of the nipple seals against an O-ring that is located in the connection. The nipple also opens the valve.

Drysuit anatomy

Inflator

In the middle of the chest with the nipple for the hose directed diagonally to the left is the usual solution.

Collar

On suits which do not have a fixed hood there is often some form of collar for holding the hood in place, reducing water circulation and keeping the neck warmer.

Exhaust valve

Older suits may have the drain valve on the forearm, but this restricts movement of the arm (or results in unwanted venting). As an automatic valve on the left upper arm avoids this problem it is now by far the most common solution.

Crotch strap

This is only used for shell suits with the zipper across the front. It allows for both greater flexibility in length and less drag underwater.

Fixed boots

The most common solution today. Normally made of some form of neoprene to contribute to insulation. Drysuit boots are normally a little larger than wetsuit boots, so ensure that your adjustable fins used for wetsuit diving fit over them.

Attached sock

Some drysuits, especially those that are made for diving in slightly warmer waters — see 'Suit choice summary' on page 40 — have a soft sock in the same material as the suit. To walk on land and wear fins, they must be supplemented with one of two solutions — see 'Boots' on page 64. There is often a short sleeve on the drysuit leg to fold over the shaft of the boot and reduce in-water drag.

Accessories for drysuits

A drysuit with fixed boots and fixed hood normally needs no additional accessories, but depending on the type of diving you will be doing there is some additional equipment that can facilitate your diving.

Hoods

In Nordic waters it is most common to have an attached hood since it provides better insulation. If your drysuit does not have an attached hood, you will need a separate one. In some instances, as when a diver has long hair, or where water temperature varies greatly through the year it can be an advantage to have a separate hood. Thinner suits made for warmer waters will have a separate hood.

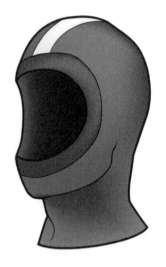

Hoods are made of neoprene as this gives the best insulation. The design of the face seal differs, but most common is neoprene with nylon lining on the outside only. This gives a good seal against the face, and the nylon lining on the outside increases durability.

Drysuits with separate hoods may have some form of collar on the suit to minimize water circulation, keep the neck warm, the hood in place and reduce water circulation.

Boots

Some shell suits have attached socks in the same material. The idea is to wear normal wetsuit boots or special drysuit 'rock boots'.

Common wetsuit boots
A good solution for most types of diving. You normally need a larger size compared with wetsuit diving because of bulky undergarments.

Rock boots
These are more rigid laced boots that provide excellent stability on land and a shape that conforms to most adjustable fins.

In the early days of drysuits many had ankle seals and separate boots, but this is unheard of now. Instead, drysuits have attached boots, so you don't have to worry about leaks in this area. Most boots also have a thick sole so you can walk comfortably on land. The disadvantage is that they can make it more difficult to don and doff fins unless you buy a pair with a little extra room.

Undersuit

As mentioned on page 52, traditional neoprene drysuits have insulating properties, but you may also need an undersuit if you really feel the cold, dive in cooler water, if the suit is thinner or if you are going deep. There are a range of fleece undersuits to suit all tastes and budgets. Some divers wear regular tracksuits.

There are also materials which *wick* sweat away from the skin, unlike cotton (which will keep moisture there). Wicking fabrics draw off liquid by capillary action. These are especially useful when surface temperature is considerably different to water temperature. Wicking undersuits, synthetic sports materials and merino wool can all be layered to achieve the desired warmth while avoiding a clammy, cold feeling.

With a membrane/shell suit, there is no insulation without an undersuit, so the water temperature and personal comfort are the key factors. The undersuit is usually a windproof jumpsuit filled with compressed fibres, much like a sleeping bag. The perceived advantage of the less bulky shell suit is most often compromised by the size of these undergarments.

The cost of undersuits is an important consideration when deciding which type of drysuit to go for. However, they do also keep you warm before and after your dives. Undersuits require regular washing to avoid developing unpleasant odours.

Gloves/mitts

Depending on water temperature, the same gloves that you use for wetsuit diving can be used with a drysuit (see page 48). Unlined neoprene gloves can seal directly onto latex wrist seals, but the seal against common lined one-piece neoprene seals is not as watertight. Semi-dry gloves with an unlined interior which seals against the skin at the wrist will keep your hands warmer.

For diving in water below around 10°C, it is more comfortable with dry gloves. There are a few different solutions for this, but the principle is — just as with a drysuit — to keep the water out. All methods involve fitting a rigid ring into the drysuit wrist. Some systems then put the collar of the glove over this ring. Alternatively, the glove is also attached to a ring and this fits into the ring located in the drysuit. Large, strong O-rings make the seal watertight. The latex or PVC gloves can be lined with fleecy material or supplemented with thin fabric gloves for warmth and comfort. Whichever system is chosen it is a simple task to replace damaged gloves, provided you carry a spare pair.

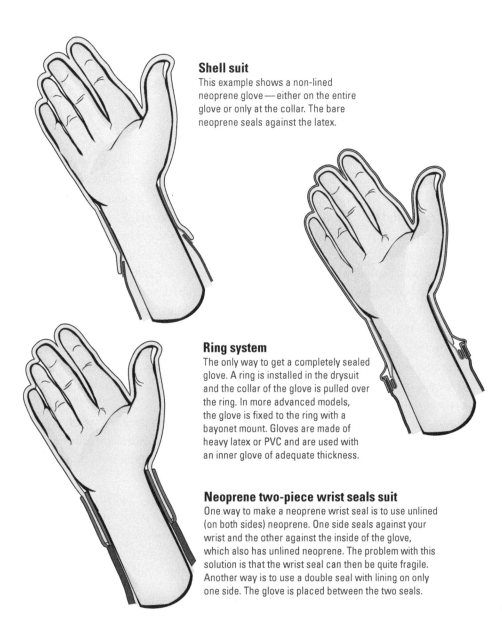

Shell suit
This example shows a non-lined neoprene glove — either on the entire glove or only at the collar. The bare neoprene seals against the latex.

Ring system
The only way to get a completely sealed glove. A ring is installed in the drysuit and the collar of the glove is pulled over the ring. In more advanced models, the glove is fixed to the ring with a bayonet mount. Gloves are made of heavy latex or PVC and are used with an inner glove of adequate thickness.

Neoprene two-piece wrist seals suit
One way to make a neoprene wrist seal is to use unlined (on both sides) neoprene. One side seals against your wrist and the other against the inside of the glove, which also has unlined neoprene. The problem with this solution is that the wrist seal can then be quite fragile. Another way is to use a double seal with lining on only one side. The glove is placed between the two seals.

Weight system

It is normal to use a common weight belt or a BCD with integrated weights when drysuit diving. An important consideration is positioning of the weights, since most people need more weight, compared to wetsuit diving. Some divers choose to use both a weight belt and integrated weights. Another solution is to use a weight harness for better distribution of the weights. They can also be fitted with accessory pockets. See *Chapter 7* on 'Weight Systems' for more information.

Pockets

Many BCDs have small or no pockets for additional accessories. For this reason, many drysuits have attached pockets or manufacturers offer this as an option.

Gaiters

One of the drysuit legends is that there is a great risk that all the air in the suit will collect at the lower legs, directly causing an uncontrolled ascent. If you have neutral buoyancy at the actual depth, it does not matter where in the suit the air is, so this is not true. However, you may be uncomfortable with too much air around your lower legs when you swim. To avoid this, you can use gaiters that restrict airflow around your calves.

Ankle weights

These are soft weights of 0.5–1 kg/1–2 lbs filled with lead shot. The idea is to keep your feet down (level with you body, as you swim horizontally) to avoid too much air getting to the lower legs. Another solution is to use heavy fins, like Jetfins.

Talcum powder

Talcum smooths your passage into and reduces strain on the seals when dressing (if seals are dry). A small amount is sufficient. Unperfumed baby powder works fine.

Weight harness

Pockets

Gaiters

Ankle weights

Maintenance

Hangers

It is important that you let your drysuit completely dry-out before storing it. Take special care of the inside. The illustrated hanger (on page 68), where the boots are inserted into two slots, allows air to circulate throughout the suit. Coat hangers, where the suit is folded over a tube do not allow this circulation.

Zip grease

Many manufacturers supply special lubricants for the zipper with their drysuits. Silicone is NOT recommended because it may be difficult to replace a broken zipper if you use it on the suit—there is no solvent which can remove it. Plastic zippers are relatively maintenance-free and only need to be lubricated at both ends. A metal zipper should be opened and then lubricated all along its *outside*. Then open and close it a few times to work the lubricant into the zip.

Beeswax

Natural beeswax is a cheap, clean and easy alternative for lubricating zips. It is available in convenient bars which can be kept in your dive bag without being damaged. Metal zippers should be opened and then lubricated all along the *outside* of the teeth. Then open and close a few times to work the wax into the zip.

Summary—Diving in a drysuit

There are many benefits to diving in drysuits, not only in very cold waters but also in more temperate ones. But it requires both thought and training, mainly due to the fact that you use the drysuit for buoyancy underwater.

Drysuit skills are not usually taught on entry-level courses, but you can find formal courses—sometimes as an offer when buying a drysuit. Diving with a drysuit is not especially difficult compared with diving in a wetsuit, but there are some other things to consider and practice—skills that you best learn through formal training. Skills that greatly reduce the possibility of a life-threatening buoyancy control issue.

Care and Maintenance

A small hole in a wetsuit is not a major problem, neither functionally or for appearance. Small tears are easy to repair with neoprene glue, while larger holes and rips in edges and seams often must be both glued and sewn, something a professional can easily do.

Most problems with wetsuits are easy to prevent. Dressing and undressing puts the most strain on seals and edges, so be careful when you put your hands and feet through. Wetsuits provide protection against scrapes and scratches. The object that could have injured you may instead damage your suit. Buoyancy control is a much better way to protect both yourself and the suit. The zipper(s) should also be lubricated occasionally for optimal function using dedicated lubricants or beeswax. Common for all neoprene suits (also drysuits) is that they should not be folded hard when stored, since the bubbles in the material can break with permanent folds as a result. Store the suit on a broad hanger instead, or roll as loosely as possible if storing in a bag.

Drysuits have more sensitive parts to care for. It is mainly the zipper and the seals around the wrists and the neck that must be carefully looked after. The zipper should be lubricated on the outside with special drysuit zipper grease or beeswax. Do not use silicone grease as this lubricant can cause problems if you need to replace the zipper as it is difficult to clean and therefore almost impossible to apply new glue to. There is no friction on the inside of the zipper, so you don't need to lubricate this side.

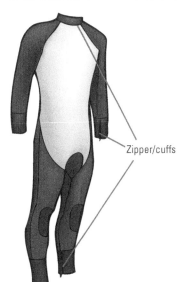

Zipper/cuffs

Wetsuit zipper/cuffs

Not all dive suits are equipped with zippers, but they do make dressing and undressing easier—especially for wrists and ankles. Full diving suits usually have a zipper at the back. Make sure you rinse zippers extra carefully. If you do not, salt deposits can build-up and make them stick. Built-up deposits can normally be removed with a weak acid solution, for example, citric acid or vinegar. If there are unlined cuffs at the wrists and/or ankles, they must be treated carefully so that they do not crack when you dress or undress. Talcum powder, lubricant or plastic bags facilitate donning if the seals are dry.

Seals on a drysuit are made of either latex, neoprene or silicone. Using talcum powder or lubricant to help ease yourself into the suit helps extend the life of latex and neoprene seals. Lubricants are not necessary with silicone ones because they are so flexible—some divers do use talcum powder though. Just be careful not to cause a puncture with your finger nails or jewellery when stretching them and do not just force your hand or head through.

Seals, especially those that are made of neoprene, should be replaced at regular intervals (when they show signs of wear), as they expand slightly with each dive. This replacement is tricky to do yourself; it is better to leave it to a professional.

Smaller punctures in a drysuit are quite easy to repair on your own, unless they are situated on or close to a seam. What you do is seal all openings in the suit (e.g. with plastic cups at the wrists and a ball at the neck), inflate it and then put some soapy water on the suspected area. The hole is where you find bubbles forming. When you have located the hole you dry the area and repair the puncture as advised by the manufacturer. After the repair, you should check your job by inflating the suit again.

The drysuit valves are another area needing attention. Both the inflation and deflation valves should be serviced regularly, for example annually or every 100 dives. Read the instructions from the manufacturer. Some valves require special tools for opening and the internal parts can be small and numerous.

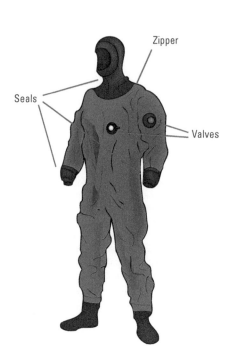

Zipper

Seals

Valves

Valves

On a drysuit, it is important that both the inflation and exhaust valves work properly. Thorough cleaning on the outside is needed, but it is important to check they function before each dive, especially if the drysuit has not been used for a while.

Zipper

The gas and watertight zipper on a drysuit is one of the most sensitive parts. It is important to be careful when closing it so that nothing gets caught, for example the undersuit. Also, store the suit either hanging up or loosely-rolled with the zipper open to facilitate ventilation and to prevent it from bending. There are special lubricants for drysuit zippers, which make it easier to open and close them. Some prefer to use a silicone spray, but if you need to replace the zipper on the suit this would make it tricky, because there are no solvents that can remove silicone.

Seals

Wash them regularly with fresh water, and inspect for cracks. A small crack can be enough to cause you to rip the seal when you put on or remove the drysuit. Use talcum powder or lubricant when you dress to reduce strain on the seals.

CHAPTER 4

Buoyancy Control Device

The animals and plants that live freely in the water all have some form of adaptation to maintain neutral buoyancy. Most bony fish have a swim bladder, sharks have a large fatty liver and some plankton have whips to prevent them from sinking. We have a BCD.

Neutral Buoyancy

Achieving correct weighting

A diver who is neutrally buoyant underwater saves energy and avoids damage to sensitive life on the bottom. Good buoyancy control starts on the surface. In your entry-level course, you learned to float with the surface level with your eyes, with a normal breath and empty BCD. Then, if when you exhale you sink you have almost the correct amount of weight: you still need to add an additional 500g/1lb to cover the air left in your cylinder This test is done at the end of a dive with a nearly empty cylinder (around 50 bar/700 psi).

Remember that the air you breathe during the dive weighs 2–3 kg/4–7 lbs. If you check on the surface with a full dive cylinder, you must add this weight, otherwise you will be positively buoyant at the end of the dive and will have difficulty controlling your ascent.

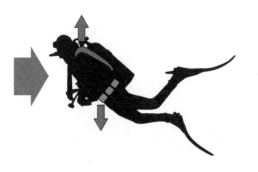

Positive buoyancy

Positively buoyant divers can only compensate by trying to swim down. If you believe you are correctly weighted and still have this problem it could be that you have excess air in your BCD, which needs to be expunged. A positively buoyant diver swimming down fighting against buoyancy uses more energy, which increases air consumption.

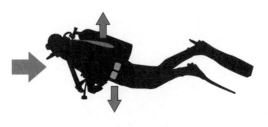

Neutral buoyancy

This is when you have done a proper weight check on the surface, don't have much air in your BCD and can swim horizontally with little effort. If you dive without a diving suit or with a short wetsuit, the weight belt might pull down your legs if you are completely still in the water. You rarely notice this imbalance when you swim forward. If you dive with a drysuit, it is possible to distribute the air in the suit so that the whole body can be perfectly balanced.

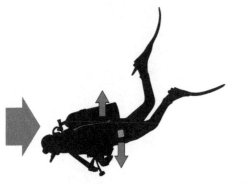

Negative buoyancy

If you have too much lead you must compensate for this by inflating your BCD. The air will pull your upper body upwards while the weights pull your hips down. This results in a swimming position with your head up and fins down. By swimming in this position you increase water resistance, which requires more effort to swim against it and therefore increases your air consumption.

Models

The buoyancy control device (BCD) is also known as a stabilizer (or shortened to 'stab jacket'), buoyancy compensator (BC), or wing (a specific type). They were introduced in the 1960s and now look quite different to the early models. The first years were dominated by horse collar BCDs. This was a major step in the development toward safer and more comfortable diving.

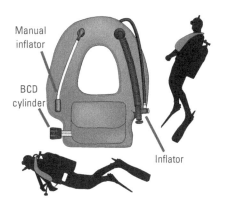

Manual inflator

BCD cylinder

Inflator

Jacket-style

Sleeveless jacket BCDs dominate the market. With the bladder both around the waist and the cylinder at the back, they give good balance horizontally underwater and vertically at the surface. With this design it is also possible to have a bladder with larger volume and therefore more potential buoyancy—a clear benefit in temperate waters with bulky drysuits and heavy weight belts.

The fit is controlled with straps at the shoulders and a cummerbund at the abdomen. Most have one or more zipped side pockets to carry small things and plastic or stainless steel D-rings for equipment like goody bags, torches or slates. There is a large choice of models, sizes and colours, so it should be easy to find one that suits you and your diving style.

Back-mounted

The first BCDs with an integrated inflator and back-pack were of this type—with the air bladder at the back—but the jacket-style won the competition back then. However, modern models have seen a rise in popularity. The reason is that the design gives more flexibility, as you can find anything from extra pockets to interchangeable wings with different buoyancy. A back-mounted BCD doesn't cover the chest as much as a jacket-style one, so many divers prefer them when drysuit diving. Another advantage is better stability underwater since you have all the buoyancy at your back—the trade off is less stability at the surface.

They are available both in models similar to the traditional jacket-style BCDs and as modular units (wing systems) that can be customized for different kinds of diving, like so-called 'technical diving' (all diving is essentially technical!). Other benefits include that your front is not covered and that they can be made lighter than traditional jacket-style BCDs.

Horse collar/assisted buoyancy life jacket (ABLJ)

A direct descendant of the inflatable life jacket, with an added hose for controlling inflation and deflation. The buoyancy was around the abdomen, so on the surface the air pressed the diver onto their back and underwater it tended to turn them away from a desirable swimming position. To keep them in place, ABLJs were fastened with a strap around the waist and one around the crotch.

Early ABLJs had manual valves. The inflator connected to the regulator first stage came later. Now only snorkelling vests have manual inflators. Some ABLJs had separate mini-cylinders for filling or as back-up. Then there was a CO_2-cartridge that could be triggered if the diver needed to quickly get to the surface. Today these are very rare options…

Jacket-style

With the air bladder on both sides of the dive cylinder—both underwater and on the surface—you get comfortable dives with good balance underwater.

Back-mounted

These can tilt you forward on the surface, so you must lean back slightly, or either breathe through your snorkel or regulator, or use your fins to compensate. But of course, we spend a limited amount of time on the surface.

Back-mounted

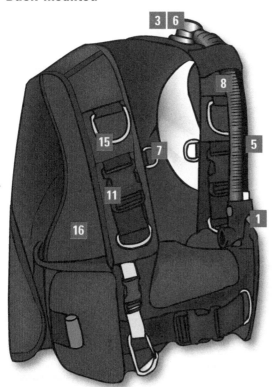

Alternate air source holders

Mouthpiece plug

Hose clip

Scumball
mouthpiece
cover

Magnetic clip

1. Inflator
The first BCDs had to be manually inflated, so this has improved diving significantly. There are many types of design and construction, but common are a button for inflation, a button for exhaust and a nipple for the connection of the low-pressure hose. Some models use different colours for the buttons.

2. Whistle
In an emergency on the surface, this is a great way to draw attention. Unfortunately, not all BCDs are sold with a whistle, but this should not be seen as an accessory but as a mandatory part.

3. Dump valve
The corrugated inflator hose is attached to the BCD at your left shoulder. The connection is combined with a quick dump valve. To dump air from your BCD on descent, you just pull the inflator. A steel cable or string inside the corrugated hose pulls open the valve. Some models also have a dump valve on the right shoulder connected via a string in a channel along the shoulder strap to a toggle which enables you to pull to open the valve.

4. Tank band
Most BCDs have one strap for attaching a cylinder, but this can be supplemented by a smaller strap at the top to stabilize it. Twin-cylinders can either be

attached with additional straps or bolted to the BCD (see page 82). Not all BCDs are suitable for using with two cylinders.

5. Low-pressure hose
This is connected to the regulator first stage and allows for quick and easy inflation of the BCD. The quick coupler for BCDs is internationally standardized, but since this has a limited air flow, there are other connections which are used for inflators with a combined function as an alternate air source. Adapters are available so a standard regulator hose can be used with different couplings. This provides a flexible solution if you own different types of BCDs.

6. Over-pressure relief valve
To protect the BCD from over-inflation, there are one or more pressure relief valves to release excessive pressure. At least one of these is usually connected to a toggle for use as a manual dump valve.

7. D-rings for chest strap
All BCDs have a strap and buckle at the abdomen. To increase stability, most BCDs also have chest straps, depending on design and intended use.

8. Corrugated inflator hose
This hose has a diameter of 15–20 mm/⅝–¾ in to allow rapid release of air from the BCD.

Jacket-style

Trigger hook/bolt snap—best

Carabiner—not as good

Inflator whistle—goes between the inflator and low pressure hose. Some come with their own hose. Most designs also work underwater. On the surface, they should be used with caution as the sound is very loud!

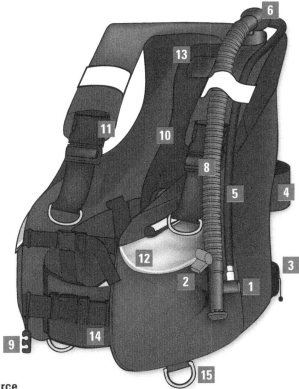

9. Holder for alternate air source

An extra second stage is the most common solution for an out-of-air problem. This is usually located on the right-hand side and attached to the BCD. You can do this in many ways (see some examples on page 74), but all ensure it is well-fixed but easy to release in an emergency.

10. Backplate

This is the same type as was previously required for diving without a BCD or with an ABLJ. Modern BCDs do not need a separate backplate since it is either integrated or there is a soft back, especially those that are made for travelling divers (because they must be light and pack down as small as possible).

11. Buckles for shoulder straps

Most modern BCDs have adjustable buckles on the shoulder straps. These facilitate simple adjustment. They are usually fitted with quick release buckles to make it easier to remove the BCD, especially useful if you need to do this in the water, e.g. to get into an inflatable boat.

12. Pockets for accessories

Depending on the type of diving, you might want to take small accessories. Or you might find some gold that you want to bring back as a memento of the dive(!). A pocket comes in handy for this.

13. Carrying handle

If the BCD is equipped with a hard backplate, there is usually a carrying handle incorporated into it. Most BCDs have a small band on the back for strapping around the cylinder's pillar valve for stability—it is not a carrying handle. A carrying handle could also be added to the dive cylinder itself. Twin tanks are lifted via the cylinder knobs/pillar valves (rather than the manifold itself).

14. Cummerbund

One or two straps with quick release buckles on the front secure the BCD, and are easily opened with one hand. For added convenience, there is usually a wide cummerbund with a Velcro fastener.

15. D-rings

Accessories which do not fit into your pockets can be attached using a variety of clips to these rings. Carabiners are less suitable for this purpose, since they can be difficult to open and could inadvertently get caught on something. Instead, use a bolt snap (also called a trigger hook).

16. Soft backplate

Many BCDs have a soft back plate, especially those that are made for travelling divers because they must be as light as possible and have little packed volume.

Wing (modular BCDs)

A wing gives the flexibility to build a perfectly-fitted streamlined unit, suited to a diver's personal preferences, type of diving and objectives (and see page 180).

1. Backplate

Generally made of aluminium (light for warm water/travel) or stainless steel (heavy for cold water) with holes for straps and attachment of the wing and dive cylinder. There are also plastic backplates. The design usually allows you to use both single and twin tanks.

2. Harness

From simple one-piece straps to models with quick-releases plus back and shoulder padding, these are infinitely adjustable. The purpose is to create a 'tailored' fit perfect for the wearer. The same backplate/harness combination can be used for single and twin tanks, though you may need to adjust it and change the wing being used.

3. Wing

The inflatable part. There is a wide range with varying characteristics: Buoyancy — sizes with lifting capacity 8–30 kg/17–65 lbs (for single, twinset or even more cylinders, warm or cold water); Safety — most have one inflator, but some wings have built-in 'redundancy' with two bladders/chambers and two inflators; Shape — can be doughnut or horseshoe, and wider wings are better adapted for twin tanks; Compression — to streamline them, some wings are

equipped with elastic cord to compress excess material when deflated so that it does not cause drag or snag on anything (the idea here is that a larger wing can be used for a greater range of purposes); and Bladder — most wings are made of a single layer of ballistic nylon, but some manufacturers make wings with an airtight inner bladder and a removable exterior protective material.

4. Crotch strap

This stabilizes the wing both on the surface and during the dive. Must be thoroughly briefed during buddy checks in case of an emergency.

5. Tank attachment

Twinsets are bolted to the back plate; singles use either the same tank band and buckle as all other types of BCDs, or a special 'single-tank adapter'. This also sandwiches the wing together.

6. Accessory pocket

Available in different models and sizes — to be attached to the harness.

7. Weight pockets

An accessory that attaches to the harness. Usually have quick dump handles and/or clips/fastenings.

Features and Construction

Inflator

We need to be able to add and release air from our BCD. In the beginning this was done by mouth, but a better and safer design using the air in the tank was soon developed. So instead of removing the regulator from the mouth, exhaling some air into the BCD, clearing the regulator, taking a few breaths (and maybe repeating the procedure) we only need to press the inflator button.

On the inflator, we also have a button to release air. This feature can also be used to manually fill the BCD with your mouth in an emergency. It is rare, but if you should experience a malfunctioning inflator or an empty tank (at the surface) you have an alternative way to gain positive buoyancy. In the past, some BCDs were equipped with a CO_2-cartridge to use in an out-of-air emergency, but unfortunately they seldom worked when needed. The mechanism was often overlooked and became corroded or the volume in the pressurised cartridge was insufficient to fill the BCD at depth. So scuba diving BCDs no longer have this option.

The inflator can also have a combined function as an alternate air source—see page 131 onwards for this and other options.

Inflator which also functions as an alternative air source

Fixing to BCD

Steel cable or string to dump valve on the shoulder

Deflation valve

Low pressure hose

Mouthpiece for manual inflation

Quick coupling

Inflation button

Deflation button

During your entry-level course you probably practiced inflating a BCD by mouth and you therefore know how much easier it is to just press the inflator button.

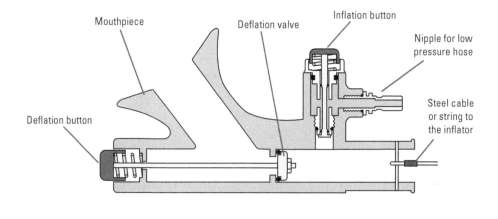

Mouthpiece   Deflation valve   Inflation button
Nipple for low pressure hose
Deflation button
Steel cable or string to the inflator

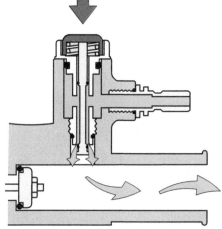

Inflation button

When you press the inflation button, you open the valve and air is allowed to pass. The internal mechanism could be of different designs, from quite large and simple parts to a Schrader valve (the same as used in car tyres and some bicycle tubes — see 'Low-pressure hose connection' on page 79).

Deflation button

The deflation button has two functions — deflation and oral inflation.

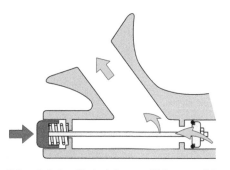

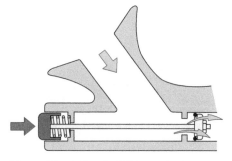

When deflating, lift the inflator as high as possible and press the deflate button.

It is possible to inflate the BCD by putting the mouthpiece to your lips, pressing the deflate button and exhaling.

Low-pressure hose connection

This connects the regulator first stage to the BCD. The quick connector is internationally standardized, but because the airflow is limited there are other types of couplings for inflators which also function as an alternative air source (see page 131 onwards).

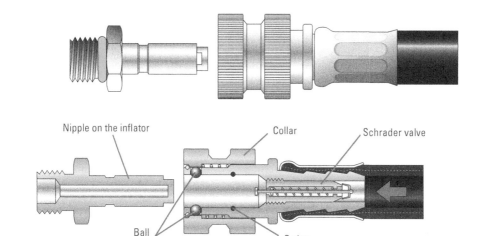

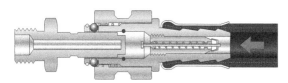

Nipple on the inflator

Collar

Schrader valve

Ball bearings

O-ring

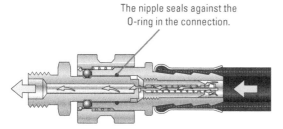

When the collar is pulled back, ball bearings move outwards and the nipple can be pushed in. When the nipple is in place, the ball bearings fall down into the groove on the nipple and the collar springs back.

The nipple seals against the O-ring in the connection.

When the quick coupling is attached, the nipple opens the valve to allow air to pass when you press the inflation button.

Leaks from the connection can either be due to a worn out O-ring or a Schrader valve in the connection not holding tight. It is cheap and easily replaced, but requires a special tool. Please note that some inflators use the alternative CEJN-connector (see page 62).

Tool for Schrader valves.

Two different types of Schrader valves.

Release valves

So, we need to be able to add air to the BCD on descent and release it during the ascent. Venting can be achieved in several ways. The most common method is to raise the inflator above the head and press the deflate button. On most BCDs you can also pull the corrugated hose that connects the inflator to the bladder. A thin stainless steel wire inside the hose then opens the quick dump valve on the shoulder. A third alternative is the over-pressure relief valve that is fitted to all BCDs to prevent ruptures due to overfilling. On some BCDs this is combined in the dump valve at the shoulder or a dump valve on the lower back.

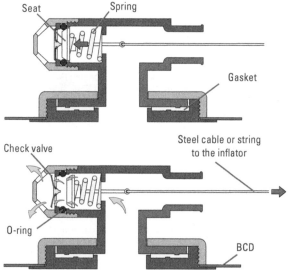

Dump valve

The corrugated inflator hose is attached to the BCD at your left shoulder. Most BCDs combine it with a quick dump valve. It may also be an over-pressure relief valve.

To vent air from your BCD, you just pull the inflator. A steel cable or string inside the corrugated hose transfers your pull to open the valve. A check valve (one-way valve) prevents water from entering the BCD.

Over-pressure relief valve

All BCDs are fitted with an over-pressure relief valve to protect the BCD from rupture in the unlikely event of inflator malfunction that results in uncontrolled filling. The valve normally sits at the right hip and has a toggle attached to it to allow manual operation.

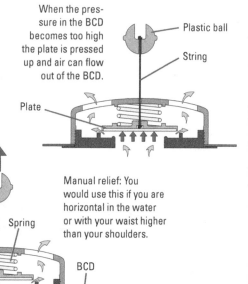

When the pressure in the BCD becomes too high the plate is pressed up and air can flow out of the BCD.

Manual relief: You would use this if you are horizontal in the water or with your waist higher than your shoulders.

Inflator with pressure relief valve

BCDs usually have a release valve on the inflator shaft to facilitate air release both at the surface and during dives. It is common that this also acts as a pressure relief valve to protect the BC against accidental overfilling.

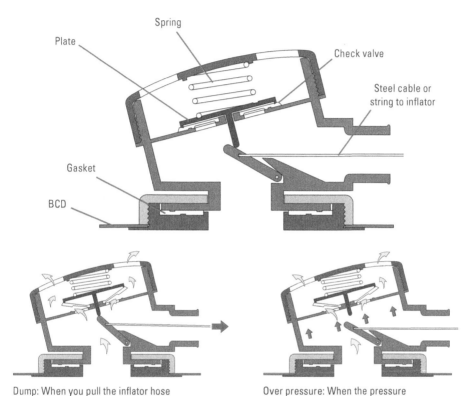

Dump: When you pull the inflator hose the wire to the valve on the shoulder opens and releases air. The check valve prevents water from entering the BCD.

Over pressure: When the pressure becomes too high the plate is pressed up and air can flow out. The check valve prevents water from entering the BCD.

Cylinder attachment

In the old days, when diving with an ABLJ, a backplate with straps held the tank. On modern BCDs this is incorporated. Some models still have a hard backpack, some have a soft back, but all models have an integrated function for fastening the tank. For all models this is a cam band — one or two straps that hold the tank with buckles. There are some different solutions for this buckle, but virtually all BCDs have the same plastic model. It does its job well, but many divers find it hard to thread and get tight enough to securely hold their cylinder. Study it carefully if you want to adjust it, so you know how to rethread it. Most BCDs also have instructions on the strap which show how to thread the band.

To attach twin tanks, there are different options. If they are *manifolded* (see page 106) you normally bolt the BCD—most likely a wing—to the steel bands that hold the two tanks together. Some BCDs can take two independent (not manifolded) tanks and use the same straps shown here, threaded through special plastic blocks between the cylinders, holding everything together. These are called twinning bands.

Tank band

Often the source of frustration, but the cam band is a simple and robust method of holding your cylinder and BCD together.

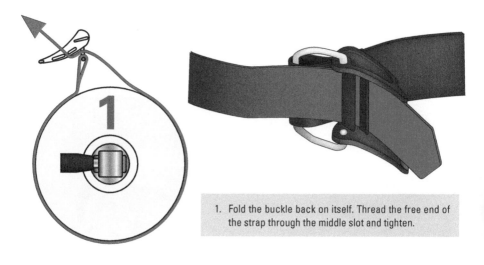

1. Fold the buckle back on itself. Thread the free end of the strap through the middle slot and tighten.

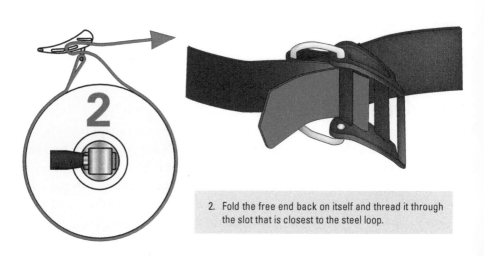

2. Fold the free end back on itself and thread it through the slot that is closest to the steel loop.

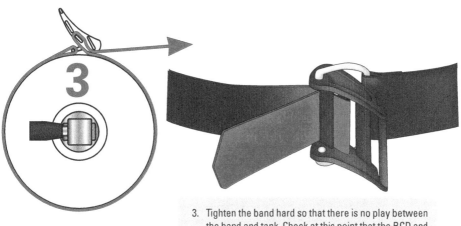

3. Tighten the band hard so that there is no play between the band and tank. Check at this point that the BCD and cylinder are aligned how you want them to be (with the pillar valve pointing at the back of the BCD).

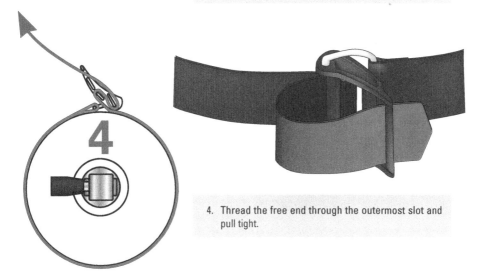

4. Thread the free end through the outermost slot and pull tight.

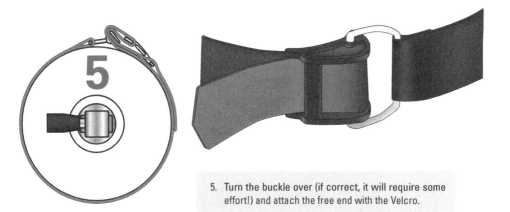

5. Turn the buckle over (if correct, it will require some effort!) and attach the free end with the Velcro.

Material

The BCD must be made of a strong material to cope with wear and tear. Some models have a bladder covered with an outer nylon shell, but most modern BCDs are made of urethane-coated nylon that are stitched or welded (or both) together to create an airtight unit. The most durable material is 1000 Denier Cordura, which makes a BCD almost impossible to wear out. Some designs use a plush material on the inside to increase friction. This makes it 'stick' to your back and reduces wear on your dive suit.

Integrated weights

Many BCDs—both back-mounted and jacket-style—have integrated weight pockets with quick dump handles. These can be more comfortable than hard weights around the waist. But they can be easier to lose when getting into or out of boats, awkward to put in and make handling the BCD harder. If you dive with a thinner wetsuit or no suit at all, you can normally put all the lead in the BCD. Due to limitations on how much the pockets can harbour, drysuit divers in colder waters often choose to put weights on a traditional weight belt or combine the two.

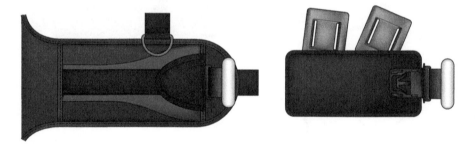

Summary

The buoyancy control device is a mandatory part of your scuba gear—you can't do without it. It combines with the dive cylinder and regulator into a convenient package that is comfortable to carry. It allows you to rest on the surface without effort and underwater to concentrate on the experience, instead of using energy to maintain your position. The invention of the BCD may not have been as great a leap forward as was the regulator, but it is a major factor in the acceptance and popularity of recreational scuba diving. Without it diving would still be a difficult sport, not the family one it is now.

Care and Maintenance

It is very rare that a modern BCD leaks due to a puncture, but if you get one you repair it in a manner similar to repairing a drysuit. The exact method depends on the model and material, so follow the manufacturer's instructions. However, it is important to realize that there could be serious consequences if the repair fails during a dive. If you are not sure of what you are doing, hand it in to your dive shop for a professional job.

More common are problems with the valves and the inflator. The over-pressure relief valve and separate dump valves should be disassembled once in a while and cleaned, especially the sealing surfaces. The low-pressure inflator is a mechanical device that is often forgotten in general maintenance. The mechanism should be rinsed after each dive by adding water to the BCD and then draining it through the inflator.

Inside
The inside of the BCD needs to be rinsed with fresh water to remove salt. Fill it with water through the inflator (while holding down the exhaust button); shake; and finish by draining via the inflator (or any of the exhaust valves).

Valves
You normally have a dump valve on the shoulder and a pressure relief valve on the back. On some BCDs the valve on the back can also be a dump valve. Check these regularly to ensure that they function as intended. Rinse thoroughly.

Inflator
It is important to flush the inflator after each day's diving. It should always be checked before each dive, so you know that it is working.

CHAPTER 5

Breathing Apparatus

Modern SCUBA was born in June 1943, so this is also the start date for recreational diving too. Jacques Cousteau and Émile Gagnan could probably not have foreseen quite how significant their invention would become. Both the scientific and the broader public would now have the opportunity to go into the amazing underwater world.

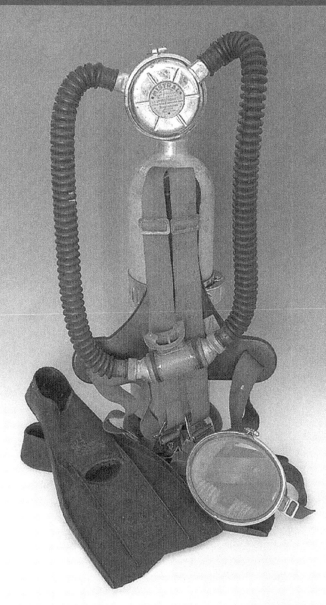

Diving equipment from the 1950s.

A Brief History

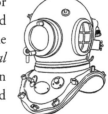

It is difficult to state who the first diver was since man's interest for what lies beneath the surface goes far back in time. The prime reason for our forefathers to dive was surely to collect food, but when this happened or where is impossible to say.

The technical utilities that were available up to the 1500s were few and did not make much difference for the diver. It was not until the 1530s, when the Italian Guglielmo de Lorena designed the first diving bell, that underwater exploration took a major step forward. Technology developed rapidly during the sixteenth century, but it would take to the latter half of the 1600s before it received a further use—salvaging goods from sunken ships.

The diving bell had its limitations for work and salvage, so it was only natural that inventive people tried to make diving less restrictive. One of these was John Lethbridge, who in 1715 designed his water-tight 'machine' that enabled him to move in a circle over the bottom. He made his living from salvaging with this apparatus for many years.

Despite many predecessors, 'modern' diving started when Augustus Siebe invented a helmet with air supplied from the surface. Now diving became a widely used tool for work underwater. Siebe had competitors, but it was during the salvaging of the man-of-war *Royal George* in Portsmouth Harbour in 1839 that Siebe's Improved Diving Dress became the most used diving system in the world.

The design also had some disadvantages in respect to freedom of movement underwater. In 1864 the Frenchmen Benoît Rouquayrol and Auguste Denayrouze designed a system that supplied the diver with air from the surface via a tank on the diver's back. In their *Aérophore* a pressure-compensating regulator controlled the air supply to the diver at ambient pressure. The principles behind this apparatus are essentially the same as those behind modern open-circuit scuba systems. However, Rouquayrol and Denayrouze had the misfortune to live in a time when it was not

possible to compress air beyond about 40 bar/ 600 psi and when there was no place for this kind of leisure activity.

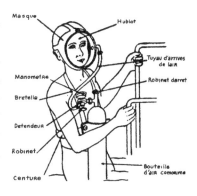

Despite the fact that they had already invented an apparatus with a pressure-compensating regulator and demand valve, in 1926 Yves Le Prieur designed an apparatus with a simple hand-operated valve to deliver air to a mouthpiece. In 1933 he added a full-face mask to avoid problems with mask squeeze. He must have been aware of the more advanced design of his compatriots, but instead he chose technical retrogression.

It was not until the Second World War, that divers got the freedom underwater that we now appreciate so much. The name Jacques Cousteau will be associated with diving and underwater exploration forever, and it was he and the engineer Émile Gagnan who in the summer of 1943 managed to develop a working apparatus of the kind we know today: self-contained and supplying air to a diver 'on demand'. The fantastic underwater world that Cousteau was able to bring to the average man sparked interest in diving. The development of diving equipment first for scientific and later for personal use increased rapidly.

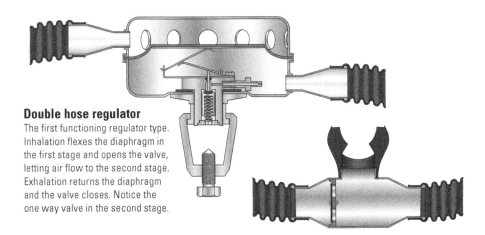

Double hose regulator
The first functioning regulator type. Inhalation flexes the diaphragm in the first stage and opens the valve, letting air flow to the second stage. Exhalation returns the diaphragm and the valve closes. Notice the one way valve in the second stage.

Technical developments from the 1960s onwards have mostly consisted in the refinement of already existing systems or designs. Many people took part in the process that has resulted in the present knowledge and equipment, and we should be grateful to them all—even if their contribution did not always immediately lead to a positive development. Their mistakes still gave us valuable knowledge.

Modern regulators do not resemble yesterday's designs at all. Progressive developments mean that they are much easier to use and breathe from and more secure than Cousteau's old double-hose regulators. This chapter explains the different design principles. The aim is not to teach you to make your own regulator with material from scrap heaps or how to service your own regulator, but to give you an understanding of how the various models work. When you choose a regulator, you must take into account the properties more than the principles. It is important that it is easy to breathe from, that it suits your type of diving and that you can get it serviced where you live.

Open-Circuit

This is the simplest type of diving apparatus and the one that most divers use. What could be easier than compressing the air we have around us into a cylinder, allowing it to flow through a breathing-controlled valve and then breathing out into the water? When the tank is empty, we just fill it again. Easy to make, easy to use, easy to learn!

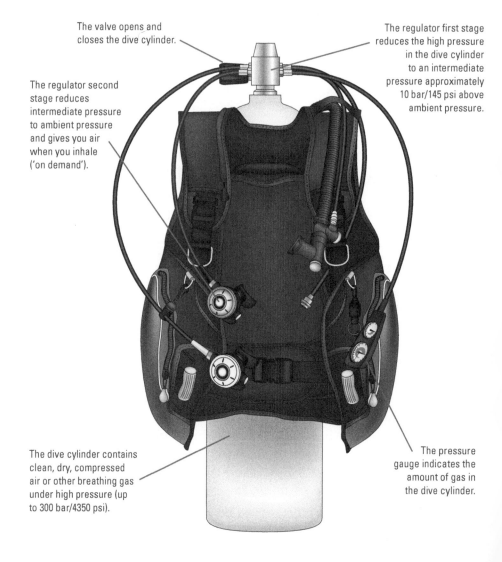

The valve opens and closes the dive cylinder.

The regulator first stage reduces the high pressure in the dive cylinder to an intermediate pressure approximately 10 bar/145 psi above ambient pressure.

The regulator second stage reduces intermediate pressure to ambient pressure and gives you air when you inhale ('on demand').

The dive cylinder contains clean, dry, compressed air or other breathing gas under high pressure (up to 300 bar/4350 psi).

The pressure gauge indicates the amount of gas in the dive cylinder.

Cylinders and Valves

The animals that live in the sea have different ways to satisfy their requirement for oxygen. Mammals and other air-breathing animals, like sea snakes and sea turtles, must surface once in a while to fill their lungs with fresh air. However, most marine animals extract oxygen directly from the surrounding water. This is not a good method for mammals like humans since we use a lot of energy to maintain our body temperature and therefore require a larger amount of oxygen. Ideas about artificial gills have been around for many years, but simple calculations show that this is hardly a reasonable alternative since they would need to be very large and move through the water at a high speed to fulfil our oxygen needs.

Instead, we have to be satisfied with taking some of the air we have around us on land with us when we dive. For this we need a container that can cope with high pressure and a valve to open and close the air supply. You don't need a technical background to realize that this is a fairly simple design, but the techniques used to manufacture high-pressure containers date only from the mid-twentieth century.

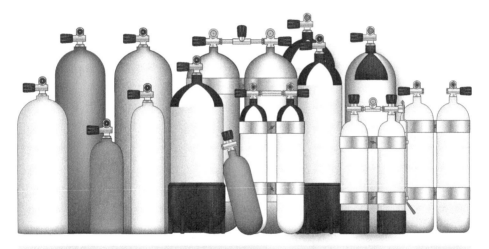

This is the trickiest section of this book to make truly international as rules and regulations concerning dive cylinders differ between countries and local dive protocols may favour different types of cylinders and configurations. So armed with this overview it is still important that you find out what applies wherever you want to dive. However, internationalization is an on-going process and the trend is for increased harmonization with fewer manufacturers and standardized sizes and models.

Despite their simplicity, we need to consider several important factors when we choose and use a scuba tank. Most of them relate to safety. A filled tank must be handled with great care because a cylinder explosion would release an enormous amount of energy. To avoid serious consequences, laws and regulations in most countries control the filling and use of high pressure vessels. Although scuba tanks are relatively small in high-pressure vessel terms, the same requirements must still be followed.

Most countries require a hydrostatic test—with certain specifications—to check the strength of the cylinder material. The time interval differs from country to country, but most common is every five years. It is also a recommendation to visually inspect the dive cylinder every year to detect corrosion at an early stage (see page 108).

Material

The first dive cylinders intended for scuba diving were made of steel, but since their introduction in the early 1970s, aluminium cylinders have increased in popularity. Aluminium is now the most common material internationally-speaking, mostly because of its durability. Experiments have been made with dive cylinders in stainless steel and different kinds of composite materials, but at the time of writing no alternative has broken the market dominance of steel and aluminium.

In a comparison between steel and aluminium cylinders, we find pros and cons for both types. Your choice depends on many factors, so there is no 'right' answer. In colder climes, however, aluminium cylinders are uncommon other than for special purposes. The table below summarises the advantages and disadvantages.

Features	Steel cylinders	Aluminium cylinders
Corrosion	Sensitive to corrosion. Galvanised both externally and internally. Painted on the outside.	A coating of aluminium oxide protects the surface. Painted only for cosmetic reasons.
Strength	Very strong material. Used for 300 bar/4350 psi.	Relatively soft metal. Max 232 bar/3300 psi.
Size	Thinner walls than aluminium tanks and therefore smaller.	Thicker walls than steel cylinders and thus larger.
Weight	Heavy both in water and on land.	Light in the water, heavy on land.
Volume	Thinner walls than aluminium cylinders and therefore less total volume.	Thicker walls than steel cylinders and hence greater volume.
Buoyancy	Negative in the water, even when empty, which means less lead needed. Especially with 300 bar/4350 psi.	Often positive in water, at least at the end of the dive.
Availability	Many models to choose from in colder climes. Less common internationally, especially in tropical climes.	A few different models to choose from. Mostly used in warmer climes, only for special purposes in colder areas.

In general terms, the only real advantage of an aluminium cylinder is that it does not corrode. It is true that aluminium is subject to corrosion, but aluminium oxide protects the material against further impact. This is the reason why dive centres in warmer climes almost exclusively use 80 cubic feet (cu ft) aluminium cylinders. The corrosive environment (high humidity) and rough handling would soon make steel cylinders unusable. However, a well-looked-after steel cylinder could give you good service for 30–40 years.

All dive cylinders must have some kind of coating to protect the surface against corrosion. Steel tanks are galvanised (sprayed with zinc) on both sides and painted on the outside. Aluminium tanks really don't need paint on the outside since they are covered with a thin layer of protective aluminium oxide. But many aluminium tanks are painted for cosmetic reasons.

Experiments have been made with a protective coating on the inside, but no such dive cylinders are on the market at the time of writing. The main problem is that even a very small puncture of the coating could result in corrosion, which would then be difficult to detect on a normal visual inspection since the coating would cover any damage.

Due to their superior buoyancy characteristics, steel cylinders are the main choice for diving outside the tropics. Aluminium cylinders are used in colder areas, but then for special purposes — stage tanks, extra tanks for bottom gas, suit gas, etc.

Pressure ratings

Most dive cylinders are made for an operating pressure of 200/232 bar (2900/3300 psi), since no aluminium tanks are made for higher pressure. This also means that most compressors are made for 200/232 bar (2900/3300 psi). In some areas with colder water, steel cylinders for higher pressure are common, for example in the Nordic countries and Germany. The main advantage with 300 bar/4350 psi cylinders is that they are heavier in water. They are also considerably heavier on land! However, it is probably reasonable to believe that 200/232 bar (2900/3300 psi) cylinders will remain the standard internationally for a long time to come.

When diving in a drysuit or thick wet suit the advantage of 300 bar/4350 psi cylinders becomes obvious. In the table on page 95 there is a comparison between different sizes, materials and pressure ratings. Note the big difference between the weights in water for the various cylinders. The more the tank weighs in water the less lead you need around your waist, and it is probably a fair assumption that most divers want as little lead as possible to haul around.

We can speculate about making tanks which can hold very high pressures, reducing the size and possibly the weight. Unfortunately, this might not be the good solution it first appears, since Boyle's Law is not linear at high pressures. We use it this way for our estimations, but Boyle's Law is only valid for an 'ideal gas'.

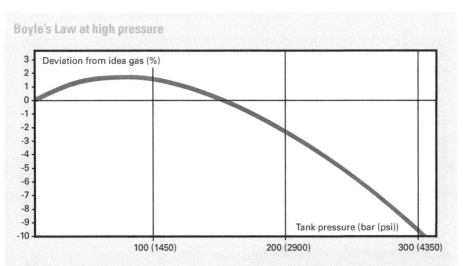

Boyle's Law states that the pressure and volume of a gas have an inverse relationship, when temperature is held constant. For air this is true within about 1% up to a pressure of 30 bar/450 psi. From 30 bar/450 psi to

100 bar/1450 psi the tank will actually contain more than what Boyle's Law predicts. The maximum is at 80 bar/1160 psi. At this pressure the tank contains 1.6% more than if air was an ideal gas. At pressures higher than 100 bar/1450 psi the molecules are pressed so close to each other that they begin to resist further compression. The result is that it becomes harder and harder to fit more air into the tank. At 200 bar/2900 psi the tank contains 2.4% less air and at 300 bar/4350 psi 9.4% less air compared with an ideal gas. So if we fill the tank to the working pressure we 'lose' some air if we use a 300 bar/4350 psi tank compared with a 200 bar/2900 psi tank. But the difference of 7% is compensated by other advantages. Also, note that these comparisons are made at 20°C. At lower temperatures the difference will decrease.

So this is something you must be aware of in speculations about future diving technology. At higher pressure than 300 bar/4350 psi, the differences get even larger. So at 600 bar/8700 psi a tank contains 30% less air than with an ideal gas and at 1000 bar/14500 psi the difference is almost 50%.

Numerical Example, Metric

A 12 litre cylinder is filled to 232 bar. It contains $12 \times 232 = 2784$ litres of air according to Boyle's Law. For an exact calculation, we must deduct 2.4% since air is not an ideal gas at this pressure. Hence, there will be 2572 litres in the cylinder. Now, it is not possible to use all of this air because we cannot suck until there is a vacuum in the cylinder. The cylinder volume will always be left, in this case 12 litres. The usable amount of air on the surface will then be 2560 litres.

How much is this in cubic feet? A cubic foot corresponds to 28.137 litres, so it will be 91 cubic feet of air.

For how long will this air last? A reasonable assumption is that we breathe approximately 25 litres of air per minute. Due to the increase in pressure, we use twice as much air at 10 metres depth, three times as much at 20 metres and four times as much at 30 metres:

10 metres: $2560 \div (25 \times 2) = 51$ minutes.
20 metres: $2560 \div (25 \times 3) = 34$ minutes.
30 metres: $2560 \div (25 \times 4) = 26$ minutes.

Numerical Example, Imperial

An 80 cu.ft cylinder is filled to 3000 psi. This actually contains only 77.4 cubic feet of air according to the manufacturer (see the table on page 95). They have probably taken into account that air is not an ideal gas when they have stated the value 77.4 cu ft. Further calculations are not necessary to find out how much air the cylinder contains, provided that the manufacturer supplies the correct information.

How much is this in litres? A cubic foot is 28.137 litres, so we will get 2178 litres. What does this correspond to in metric cylinder size? 3000 psi is 207 bar, 2178 divided by 207 is 10.5 litres.

For how long will this air last? A reasonable assumption is that we breathe approximately 0.85 cubic foot per minute. Due to the increase in pressure, we use twice as much air at 33 feet depth, three times as much at 66 feet and four times as much at 99 feet:

33 feet: $77.4 \div (0.85 \times 2) = 46$ minutes.
66 feet: $77.4 \div (0.85 \times 3) = 30$ minutes.
99 feet: $77.4 \div (0.85 \times 4) = 23$ minutes.

You can reduce your air consumption by being in good physical condition and streamlined, neutrally buoyant (see page 72) and calm underwater.

Sizes

You will find two different ways to show the size of a scuba tank. The metric method is to give the empty volume in litres (water capacity). Boyle's Law then gives us the method to work out the amount of air at different pressures. Standard sizes for 200/232 bar (2900/3300 psi) dive cylinders are 10, 12 or 15 litres. Twin tanks with 2×7, 2×8.5, 2×10 and 2×12 litres are also available. For 300 bar/4350 psi you find 3, 7, 8, 10 and 12 litre single tanks and twin tanks with 2×4, 2×7, 2×8.5, 2×10 and 2×12 litre. Availability varies from country to country.

The second method is imperial with the tank rated according to the amount of free air in cubic feet (cu ft) at the nominal working pressure. Common sizes are 63, 80 and 100 cu ft See the table below for a comparison between different tank sizes.

Specifications of standard sizes of cylinders

Size	Material	Working pressure		Capacity		Weight on land				Weight in water				Diameter		Length	
						Empty		Full		Empty		Full					
		bar	psi	litre	ft³	kg	lbs	kg	lbs	kg	lbs	kg	lbs	mm	in	mm	in
7	Steel	232	3365	1624	57.3	7.7	16.8	9.8	21.6	-1.0	-2.2	-3.0	-6.6	140	5.50	605	23.8
8.5	Steel	232	3365	1972	70	10.5	23.1	13.1	28.8	-1.1	-2.4	-3.5	-7.6	140	5.50	710	28.0
10	Steel	232	3365	2320	82	12.0	26.4	14.7	32.3	-1.0	-2.2	-4.0	-8.8	178	7.00	560	22.0
12, short	Steel	232	3365	2784	98	14.2	31.3	18.5	40.6	-1.5	-3.3	-5.0	-11.0	204	8.00	515	20.3
12, long	Steel	232	3365	2784	98	12.9	28.4	16.8	36.9	-0.8	-1.7	-4.2	-9.4	178	7.00	625	24.6
15	Steel	232	3365	3480	136	16.5	36.4	21.5	47.2	-1.0	-2.2	-5.2	-11.6	204	8.00	610	24.0
18	Steel	232	3365	4176	147	22.4	49.4	29.1	64.1	-0.8	-1.7	-5.8	-12.7	204	8.00	715	28.1
7	Steel	300	4350	2100	74	8.6	18.9	11.3	24.9	-1.5	-3.3	-4.2	-9.3	140	5.50	615	24.2
8,5	Steel	300	4350	2550	90	10.1	22.2	13.4	29.5	-1.4	-3.1	-4.7	-10.4	140	5.50	725	28.5
10	Steel	300	4350	3000	106	15.5	34.1	19.4	42.7	-4.5	-9.9	-8.4	-18.5	171	6.73	620	24.4
12	Steel	300	4350	3600	127	17.9	39.4	22.6	49.7	-5.1	11.2	-9.8	-21.5	171	6.73	725	28.5
50	Alu	207	3000	1371	48.4	9.6	21.2	12.5	27.5	+0.36	+0.8	-1.04	-2.3	175	6.90	483	19.0
63	Alu	207	3000	1784	63	12.1	26.1	15.6	34.5	+0.77	+1.7	-1.0	-2.2	184	7.25	556	21.9
72	Alu	207	3000	2038	72	12.6	27.8	16.4	36.0	+1.3	2.8	-0.8	-0.7	175	6.89	660	26.0
80	Alu	207	3000	2178	77.4	14.2	31.4	18.8	41.5	+1.54	+3.4	-0.64	-1.4	184	7.25	663	26.1
60	Alu	228	3300	1670	60	12.4	27.3	16.1	35.4	-0,8	-1.8	-2.5	-5.6	184	7.25	506	19.9
80	Alu	228	3300	2178	77.4	16.1	35.4	20.9	46.0	+0.41	+0.9	-2.59	-5.7	184	7.25	665	25.8
100	Alu	228	3300	2798	98.8	18.6	41	24.1	53.2	+0.86	+1.9	-1.95	-4.3	203	8.00	665	26.2

This compilation is based on manufacturer data. Unfortunately, there is no uniform system to state characteristics for dive cylinders:

1. Weight can be stated both with and without valve.
2. Buoyancy is usually stated for salt water, some manufacturers do not specify.
3. Most manufacturers of aluminium cylinders indicate buoyancy for an empty cylinder at 500 psi/35 bar, which means that the cylinder contains approximately 0.5 kg/1.1 lbs air.

So, the table data should not be taken as an absolute truth, but as an aid to see the general differences between different materials, sizes and working pressures.

There are a number of different types of dive cylinders still in circulation with other sizes, but these will be phased out. For example steel cylinders up to 200 bar/2900 psi (there is the newer standard 232 bar/3364 psi). Small cylinders for special purposes, such as pony-bottles and suit cylinders, have not been included.

The manufacturing of dive cylinders is concentrated in a few international companies, which will most likely mean that the supply of various types and models will reduce, and that we will see international harmonization:

Steel—Faber (Italy) and Eurocylinders (Germany).

Aluminium —Luxfer (USA and UK), Catalina (USA) and Worthington (Canada).

The most common dive cylinders for recreational diving are aluminium 80 cu ft and steel 12 litre. Not too many years ago, the type of compilation shown on page 95 would not have contained so many large cylinders and twin sets, but technical diving (and safety) has driven the development toward greater gas supplies. There are, however, few divers who actually need 6000 litres/212 cu ft of breathing gas during a dive.

Most dive cylinders are specified according to DOT (Department of Transportation, USA), TC (or CTC, Transport Canada) and the EU with the CE marking (PED, Pressure Equipment Directive 97/23/EC, CE0038).

Markings

All high-pressure vessels must be marked with certain information to avoid mix-ups and confusion that can lead to injury or damage. The rules vary by country, so the following are merely examples of the most frequently used markings. Please also note that there are older dive cylinders on the market that are manufactured in accordance with other standards.

European steel tank

M25×2 — Thread for the valve.

EN144—Manufacturing standard for the neck and thread.

CE0038—Shows that the bottle is manufactured in accordance with EU directives.

I—Country of manufacture (Italy).

Faber—Manufacturer.

12/2074/039—Serial number so that the cylinder can be traced.

UT 4.8 mm—Minimum wall thickness.

BS5045/7/CM/S—National standards for pressure vessels, in this case British standard for pressure vessels between 0.5 and 15 litres. Not all countries within the EU have national standards or require this, instead the CE marking is sufficient.

WT 14.2 kg—The cylinder tare weight without valve.

V12.2 L—Water capacity in litres.

PS 232 BAR AT 15°C—Working pressure at 15°C. Should not be exceeded.

PT 348 BAR—Hydrostatic test pressure.

TS-50 +60°C—Permissible pressure increase at 60°C (50 bar).

2014/10—Original test date at the time of manufacture. Subsequent test dates will be stamped on the cylinder, together with the test facility's unique mark.

European aluminium tank

M25×2—Thread for the valve.
EN144—Manufacturing standard for the neck and thread.
CE0038—Tank manufactured in accordance with EU directives.
UK—Country of manufacture.
Luxfer—Manufacturer.
P3173V/ 2537A—Serial number so that the cylinder can be traced if problems occur.
AA6061 T6—Designation for used alloy.
UT 11.6 mm—Minimum wall thickness.
WT 14.7 kg—The cylinder tare weight without valve.
V11.1 L—Water capacity in litres.
PW 232 BAR—Working pressure, not to be exceeded.
PT 348 BAR—Hydrostatic test pressure.
PS 287 BAR AT 60°—Maximum pressure and temperature the cylinder has been designed for.
2014/10—Original test date at the time of manufacture. Subsequent test dates will be stamped on the cylinder, together with the test facility's unique mark.

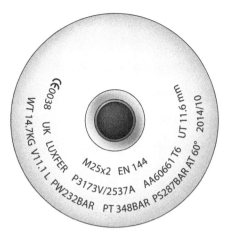

North American steel tank (high pressure)

TC—Transport Canada.
SU4957—Special permission for this rating, Canada.
230—Working pressure, bar.
DOT—US Department of Transportation.
14157—Special permission for this rating, United States.
3442—Working pressure, psi.
M8000—Identification number of manufacturing factory.
REE 75.3—Rejection Elastic Expansion, maximum permissible expansion in the hydrostatic test. If the cylinder exceeds this it may not be used.
X7 100—Manufacturer's model designation.
4403467—Serial number.
TP5250—Hydrostatic test pressure, psi.
1 Δ 10—Month and year of manufacture and the independent inspector mark between. After later successful hydrostatic tests a corresponding mark will be made.
XYZ Scuba—Distributor.

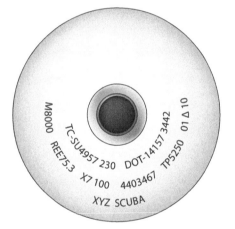

North American steel tank (low pressure)

TC—Transport Canada.
3AAM—Designation for used alloy, Canada.
DOT—US Department of Transportation.
3AA—Designation for used alloy, United States.
184/2400—Working pressure, bar/psi.
M8000—Identification number of manufacturing factory.
REE 62—Rejection Elastic Expansion (see above).
LP 85—Manufacturer's model designation.
6703467—Serial number.
01 Δ 10—Month/year of manufacture and independent inspector mark between. After later successful tests a similar mark will be made.
+-—Indicates that the bottle was found in good condition when tested, so may be overfilled by 10% of the working pressure, then 193 bar/2520 psi. This assessment is made at each hydrostatic test.
XYZ Scuba—Distributor.

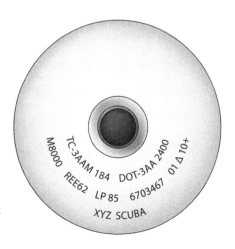

North American aluminium tank

TC — Transport Canada.
3ALM — Designation for used alloy, Canada.
DOT — US Department of Transportation.
3AL — Designation for used alloy, United States.
207/3000 — Working pressure, bar/psi.
S080 — Manufacturers model number.
R4905730 — Serial number.
Luxfer — Manufacturers name.
5 Δ 10 — Month and year of manufacture and the independent inspector mark between. After later successful hydrostatic tests a corresponding marking will be made.

North American older steel tank, LP

DOT — US Department of Transportation.
CTC — Transport Canada (the same as TC on newer bottles).
3AA — Designation for use steel alloy, United States.
2250 — Working pressure, psi.
HJ338766 — Serial number.
PST — Manufacturer's name (in this case Pressed Steel).
5 Δ 98 — Month and year of manufacture and the independent inspector mark between. After later successful hydrostatic tests a corresponding mark will be made.
+· — The bottle is found in good condition when tested, so it is allowed to be overfilled up to 10% of the working pressure, then 193 bar/2520 psi. This assessment is made at each hydrostatic test.
XYZ Scuba — Distributor.

Older cylinders

Older steel cylinders can have the following markings. The example shows manufacturer (IWKA) and the serial number on the first row. Second row shows test and filling pressure. Third row shows volume, breathing gas, weight, and date of hydrostatic test with the test facility's unique mark.

IWKA H348872
PT.TR 450 BAR   FYLLN. TR 300 BAR
RYMD 10L   LUFT   13.96KG   3 ⬦ 98

Anatomy of a dive cylinder

The production and construction characteristics of aluminium and steel cylinders are quite different. Production requires large investment, so there are only a few manufacturers worldwide. Informative films about the manufacturing process for both aluminium and steel cylinders are readily available on YouTube.

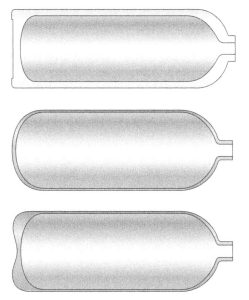

Aluminium cylinder

The common aluminium cylinder has a flat bottom and slightly thicker material at the top and bottom. Walls are approximately 12 mm thick. In spite of the fact that steel has almost three times the density of aluminium, an aluminium cylinder weighs about as much as a steel cylinder with the same capacity. However, the thicker material gives a larger external volume and therefore significantly greater buoyancy compared with a steel cylinder.

Normal steel cylinder

A normal steel cylinder has a round bottom (usually concealed by a rubber boot) and slightly thicker material at the top and bottom. Walls approximately 5 mm thick.

Steel cylinder with concave bottom

This is a newer type of steel cylinder. The advantage is that they can stand upright without a plastic boot and that they are heavier in the bottom compared to standard steel cylinders — which provides better balance underwater.

Other breathing gases

Most dives are still done with standard compressed air. The only alteration to the air is that it is dried before filling to avoid internal corrosion of the cylinder. However, more and more dives are being made with gas mixtures other than air, so it is important to know what the bottle contains in order to avoid serious incidents. This is the reason why cylinders must be colour-coded and/or properly labelled.

Air is a relative concept because the relationship between oxygen and nitrogen can vary. Breathing mixtures with a higher fraction of oxygen are called oxygen-enriched air or enriched air nitrox and these cylinders should be marked with a green-yellow sticker.

Argon is sometimes used for the suit when drysuit diving. Helium is an element in Trimix, which is a mixture of oxygen, nitrogen and helium (see *Chapter 9*).

As already mentioned, there are many different local rules and protocols regarding dive cylinders. It is therefore important that you complement what is written here with the information that applies in your area. The vast majority of all the dives that are made in the world are done with a rented dive cylinder at a scuba diving centre—most likely an 80 cu ft aluminium cylinder.

There is no international standard for colour-coding of dive cylinders, even if attempts have been made to achieve one. It is better to rely on the sticker stating the gas mixture. In Europe, a UN number indicates this and gas bottles follow *EN 1089-3: Transportable gas cylinders: Gas cylinder identification* (the colours in the image below), but this regulatory framework is not mandatory. Please note that this standard only provides for colour on the shoulder (top) of the bottle. The rest can be any colour. In the United States there are no corresponding national standards regulating colour coding and transport.

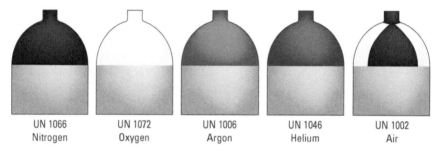

| UN 1066 | UN 1072 | UN 1006 | UN 1046 | UN 1002 |
| Nitrogen | Oxygen | Argon | Helium | Air |

In Europe, the sticker should also contain transportation information, regulated in the European Agreement concerning the International Carriage of Dangerous Goods by Road. Dive cylinders are regarded as dangerous goods (where the pressure is the danger). Individuals are exempted from the requirements if the cylinders are intended for personal/sport/leisure use. The amount carried should be reasonable for personal use.

Pillar valves

To be able to use a tank it must have a valve to open and close it. The valve must also have a connection you can attach a regulator to.

Connections

There are two types of connection between valve and regulator. Most common internationally is the yoke valve (A-clamp). As the name implies, it is a yoke that clamps over the valve. The O-ring sits *in the valve*. This type is only approved for pressures up to 232 bar/3300 psi. In northern Europe the DIN connector is the most common type, and it is becoming increasingly popular among technical divers internationally. The DIN-coupling is available in three versions—for 200 bar/2900 psi, 300 bar/4350 psi and nitrox/trimix (see 'DIN variants' on page 104). Here, the O-ring is seated *in the regulator*. It is possible to buy yoke adapters if you have a DIN regulator and are planning a dive holiday to warmer latitudes—but check ahead whether this is needed. Many manufacturers make their valves to suit both yoke and DIN regulators—they have a insert that can easily be removed using an hex (Allen) key.

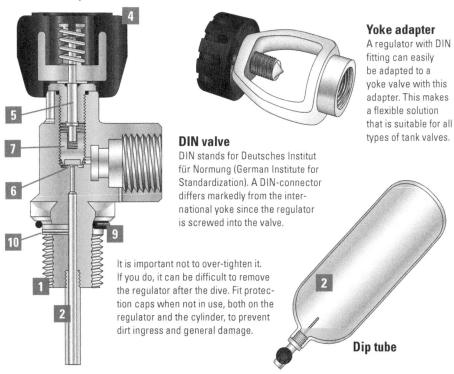

Yoke adapter

A regulator with DIN fitting can easily be adapted to a yoke valve with this adapter. This makes a flexible solution that is suitable for all types of tank valves.

DIN valve

DIN stands for Deutsches Institut für Normung (German Institute for Standardization). A DIN-connector differs markedly from the international yoke since the regulator is screwed into the valve.

It is important not to over-tighten it. If you do, it can be difficult to remove the regulator after the dive. Fit protection caps when not in use, both on the regulator and the cylinder, to prevent dirt ingress and general damage.

Dip tube

1. Threads

The valve is screwed tight to the cylinder. In Europe, the threads are standardized to M25×2, but there are some other threads on older dive tanks, e.g. conical thread. North American and older British dive cylinders use other threads—usually 3/4 NPS. This and the M25×2 are very similar, so it is important that the valve is easy to screw in to the cylinder. It is not until it comes down to the O-ring that you feel any resistance. It is possible to install a valve with the wrong threads using force, but this can cause serious damage!

2. Dip tube

This tube protects the valve and regulator in the unlikely event of water or loose particles getting into the dive cylinder. If the cylinder moves up and down (which is not unlikely when you dive), these unwanted things won't become trapped in the valve or regulator and interfere with the supply of air.

3. Insert

Many manufacturers make tank valves to fit both yoke and DIN couplings. They have an insert that is removed in order to use a DIN regulator.

4. Hand wheel

All valves have a right-hand thread, which means that you open counter-clockwise and close clockwise.

5. Stem

This transmits the rotation of the hand wheel to the seat assembly.

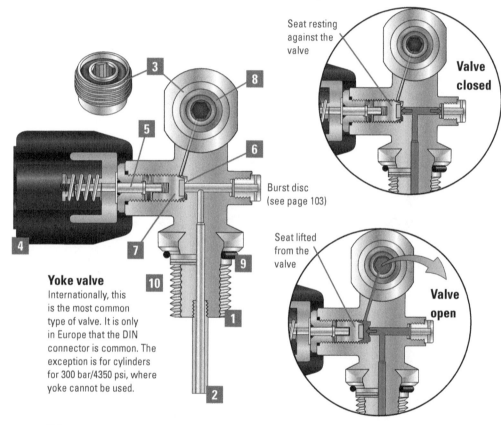

Seat resting against the valve

Valve closed

Burst disc (see page 103)

Seat lifted from the valve

Valve open

Yoke valve
Internationally, this is the most common type of valve. It is only in Europe that the DIN connector is common. The exception is for cylinders for 300 bar/4350 psi, where yoke cannot be used.

6. Lower seat

The lower seat is a raised edge in the valve that the plastic insert in the brass plug seals against. It is important that the surface is clean and free of scratches.

7. Seat assembly

This is a threaded brass plug with a slot for the stem and a plastic insert that seals against a ridge in the valve. As you have probably noticed from using one, you do not move the hand wheel in or out when you turn it; the longitudinal movement takes place inside the valve where the stem turns the seat assembly. When you turn off the valve, it is important not to over-tighten it to avoid damaging the sealing surface. During valve servicing, it is essential to replace the seat assembly, together with the O-rings and Teflon washers.

8. O-ring

With a yoke connector, the O-ring is located in the valve. It is important to check this before you put the regulator in place. It is a good idea to carry a few spare O-rings.

9. O-ring

This O-ring is normally replaced at the internal inspection and hydrostatic test. It does not wear but is deformed by the high pressure. Since this is the only seal between the cylinder and the valve, it is important that it does not leak.

10. Bypass channel

It is possible to unscrew the valve with force even if there still is a small excess pressure in the cylinder. The bypass channel releases the pressure to avoid damage to the threads and to prevent the valve shooting out with force when the thread no longer holds. This safety feature is not available on all tank valves. If you decide to remove a valve, you should make sure that the cylinder is completely depressurized and that the valve is easy to unscrew.

> **A half turn back?...**
>
> You might have learned in your entry-level course that the pillar valve should be opened completely and then back half a turn to prevent it from getting stuck in the open position. This recommendation has since been revised as modern tank valves don't stick and following the procedure can introduce some risk. If you enter the water with a tank valve fully closed, at most you will get one breath of air when you inhale. Most likely you will still be on the surface when this happens or at most only a metre or so down. A tank valve opened just a quarter turn will allow the regulator to function at the surface, but will become harder to deliver enough volume at depth mimicking a regulator failure. Switching to your octopus will not help. The diver might then only have the option of an emergency ascent.

Burst disc

This is a safety device which, if the cylinder is over-filled or if it is exposed to high temperatures (where the gas in the bottle expands), will rupture and let gas leak out.

Since the burst disc deforms during use, especially if the cylinder is overfilled, it is important to replace it regularly. This should be done during an internal inspection or hydrostatic test.

If the burst disc ruptures during filling or on the way to a dive site, it creates in the best case only discomfort, but the rapid pressure release can put a cylinder in motion.

Internationally, tank valves with a burst disc are unusual, but in North America it is a requirement for all high-pressure cylinders.

A burst disk is a calibrated disk made of copper or stainless steel, and its thickness

Burst disc

Bolt with two or more channels

Teflon washer

Use deforms the burst disc

Fatigue or excessive pressure make the burst disc break

determines at what pressure it will break—it should normally be about the same as the test pressure for the dive cylinder.

At installation, it is important to use the correct tightening torque—too loose and it will not seal, too hard and it can break at lower pressure than intended.

DIN variants

DIN connectors are available in two main variants—one for 200 bar/2900 psi and one for 300 bar/4350 psi, where the latter is longer (has more threads). This means that a DIN connector for 200 bar/2900 psi will not seal in a valve made for 300 bar/4350 psi. Virtually all DIN regulators sold now have the 300 bar/4350 psi standard.

There is also a relatively new standard for dive cylinders intended for nitrox and trimix, which has a larger diameter than the standard DIN thread—M26. Bureaucrats in Brussels felt that it is important to have different connections for different gas mixtures to avoid accidental use of the wrong gas. This new standard does not seem to have had any major impact in the industry at the time of writing.

Standard valve (K-valve)

This is a simple on/off valve to open and close the air supply, like the ones illustrated on the previous pages. The design differs between manufacturers, but the basic principle is the same. You will also find many modular designs, like twin tank manifolds, H-valves, etc. (see page 106).

Reserve valve (J-valve)

The reserve valve is now rare and only used in certain circumstances. It is a standard valve that has been fitted with a mechanism that closes the air supply at about 50 bar/750 psi. It does not give you more air; it just tells you that it is about time to return to the surface, so it is not a replacement for a pressure gauge but complements it. Professional divers working in zero visibility have a genuine use for this product. Dive cylinders that are sold for recreational diving have the standard K-valve.

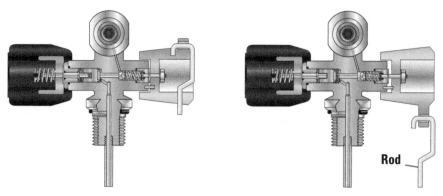

Rod

Opening and closing operates in the same way as a K-valve but when the pressure in the dive cylinder drops to the set value, you notice increased breathing resistance. When you pull the rod to open the reserve, you can use the last air in the normal way.

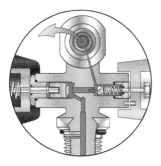 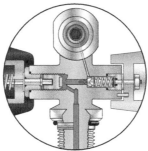 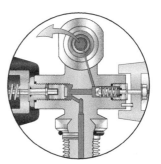

Open

Tank pressure affects a spring-loaded valve—if it is higher than a preset value it opens and the air flows from the tank to the regulator.

Closed

The valve closes the air supply when the pressure in the cylinder is less than the spring tension.

Rod pulled

The rod allows you to open the reserve valve, so that the remaining air can be used.

Reserve valve—twinset

The reserve is located on one of the cylinders, so this valve is designed differently to one for single tanks.

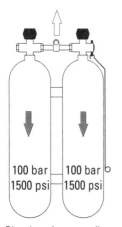 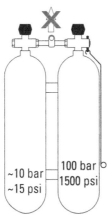 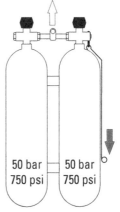

100 bar 1500 psi	100 bar 1500 psi	
~10 bar ~15 psi	100 bar 1500 psi	
50 bar 750 psi	50 bar 750 psi	

Diver breathes normally down to approximately 100 bar/1450 psi.

The valve closes at approximately 100 bar/1450 psi. Diver continues to breathe from the other cylinder until it is almost empty.

When the rod is pulled, air is distributed between both cylinders and diver ends the dive.

Y-valves and H-valves

These designs allow the diver to have two independent regulator systems on a single cylinder. If one regulator begins freeflowing, it can be shut off from the air supply while you continue to breathe from the other regulator. The set-up requires two first stages with at least one second stage on each. This solution is not unusual among divers exploring places where there is no direct access to the surface, for example, cave diving and wreck diving but now sidemount, twinsets or closed-circuit rebreathers are the preferred methods—see *Chapter 9.*

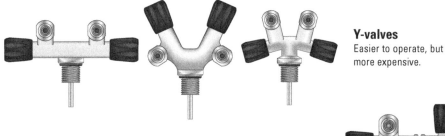

Y-valves
Easier to operate, but more expensive.

H-valves
Modular since the main valve set is a part of a manifold—you choose left or right.

Twinsets

Twinned-tanks provide many advantages—you *can* have two completely independent air supplies, you have more breathing gas and all in a comfortable package which distributes weight on the back to give you better balance in the water. Twin tanks are also more negatively buoyant in the water, which is an advantage for drysuit diving. Twinsets are held together with steel bands, but on some BCDs you can use twinning bands with two independent cylinders (see page 81).

Manifold with isolating valve

Requires two separate regulators and allows you to use both dive cylinders simultaneously. Should one of the regulators freeflow, you first close the isolation valve (centre), then the valve to the freeflowing regulator and finally you reopen the isolating valve. Your dive is terminated with the remaining air from both cylinders. This requires that you are trained in the manoeuvre to close and open the valves quickly—especially to close the isolating valve. Otherwise, there is a great risk that you will lose a lot of air.

Manifold but no isolating valve

Requires two separate regulators and allows you to use both cylinders simultaneously. Should one regulator freeflow, you close the valve to this regulator and end the dive with air from both cylinders. This is almost the same solution as the kit with an isolating valve, but because it can be difficult to find and access the correct valve to close in an emergency, it means that there is a risk of losing a lot of air.

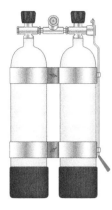

Reserve valve twinset

This set up uses one regulator, so you do not have two independent air sources, but still have the other advantages of twin tanks.

Separate cylinders

Here we have two separate regulators, but no connection between the cylinders. If one regulator malfunctions the air in the other cylinder is not affected. Before you turn off the valve to the free-flowing regulator, you only lose air from that cylinder. The disadvantages are that to use both cylinders you need to switch regulators underwater, and you must have and monitor two pressure gauges.

Accessories

Rubber boots are a normal addition to steel cylinders since most have round bottoms and therefore do not stand up well without support. Aluminium cylinders have flat bottoms, so do not need boots.

To protect the cylinder against wear many divers fit a net or mesh, but you must not cover the markings. A handle is also a good investment, making the cylinder much easier to carry.

A check gauge makes it easier to measure the pressure. If you have several dive cylinders and only dive sporadically, it is especially important to check the pressure before you travel to the dive site, although you can also do this by attaching a regulator set which includes a pressure gauge.

Boot

Should be removed occasionally to check for corrosion. Makes it difficult to wash off all salt water and will dry slower underneath.

Net

It is not common to use a net on an aluminium cylinder, but steel cylinders ought to be protected against knocks and bumps. Just make sure that it is possible to read the markings on the neck!

Handle

Tanks are quite heavy, so a good handle helps with carrying. Twinsets usually have a natural handle created between the tanks. However, despite its strength, some say that carrying large twinsets by the manifold should not be recommended.

Check pressure gauge

This is the same type of pressure gauge that is fitted to most regulators, but without a hose. Instead, you have the same connection to the tank valve as your regulator. If you only dive with yoke regulators you need, of course, only this type of connection, but one that is fitted with a DIN connection can be used for both systems if you have a yoke adapter, just as the regulator can. There must be a bleed screw to relieve the pressure and enable you to remove the gauge from the cylinder.

Care and maintenance

For the dive cylinder, our concerns are not only the investment, but also what the law requires. Most countries have regulations stipulating the time interval between hydrostatic tests, normally three to five years depending on material. On a hydrostatic test the strength of the material in the tank is checked and a visual inspection performed. The date (year and month) of the latest test is always stamped on the tank neck. The test centre will normally service the valve at the same time. To avoid problems with the valve, it is important to not tighten it too hard when you close it since this will soon damage the seal. So, always carry spare O-rings.

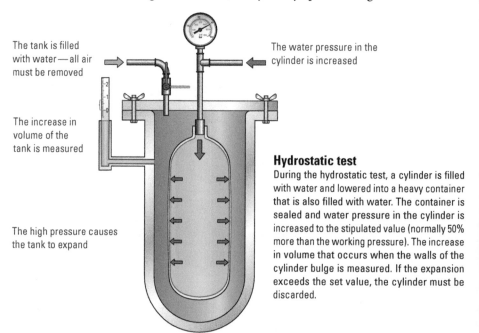

The tank is filled with water—all air must be removed

The water pressure in the cylinder is increased

The increase in volume of the tank is measured

The high pressure causes the tank to expand

Hydrostatic test

During the hydrostatic test, a cylinder is filled with water and lowered into a heavy container that is also filled with water. The container is sealed and water pressure in the cylinder is increased to the stipulated value (normally 50% more than the working pressure). The increase in volume that occurs when the walls of the cylinder bulge is measured. If the expansion exceeds the set value, the cylinder must be discarded.

It is also a common recommendation to perform an annual visual inspection (inside and outside). In the UK this is required every two and a half years with or without the hydrostatic test, but at time of going to press it was not clear whether the new international standard ISO 18119—requiring annual visual inspections—would be enforced.

During a visual inspection corrosion can be detected in time to save expensive corrective measures, or maybe even scrapping. A qualified professional must do this inspection since it needs special equipment and specifications from the manufacturer about tightening torque, etc.

Corrosion on the inside of the tank is normally due to moisture, so it is important to only fill with dry air and to never empty it completely. Always fill your tank from a well-maintained compressor. Moisture can also enter if there is a small amount of water in the valve when it is connected to the filling ramp, so always bleed the valve for a few seconds before it is connected. Corrosion can form even if you don't use it for a while, the higher the pressure, the bigger the risk. So if you want to store the tank for a long period, never have more than 20–30 bar/300–500 psi in it.

Visual inspection

It is a strong recommendation that the dive cylinder is regularly inspected on the outside and the inside. In some countries this is a requirement. Normally, the hydrostatic test requirement is every fifth year, so during this time a lot can happen.

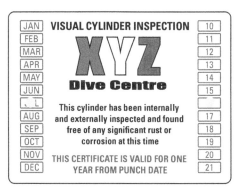

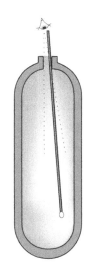

The outside of the tank is easier to inspect yourself. Inspect it regularly to see if there are any signs of corrosion. A tank net only gives good protection against small hits. If you detect signs of corrosion, you should remove it with fine sand paper and cover the area with anti-rust paint, then paint of the same colour as the tank. Note that if you make any changes that can weaken the material like sand blasting or heat painting, you must hand it in for a new hydrostatic test.

Most tanks have a boot made of rubber or plastic. Unfortunately, most divers forget to rinse the tank under the boot. The salt and moisture which accumulates under the boot is a common source of corrosion. So it is important to remove the boot regularly to rinse the area. Let everything dry completely before you assemble the parts again. This is especially important if the tank has a protective net. This discussion of corrosion mainly applies to steel tanks. Aluminium is not as prone to these problems as steel tanks.

Net

It is not common to use a protecting mesh or net on aluminium cylinders. Steel cylinders are much more susceptible to corrosion, so a protection on the outside against knocks and bumps will help prevent rust. Just make sure that it is possible to read the markings!

Handle

A dive cylinder is quite heavy, so a good handle helps when you carry it. This should only apply to single tanks, as twinsets have a natural handle between the two tanks. However, although manifolds are very strong many divers consider it too great a risk to use them, especially with heavier twinsets.

Boot

If you have a steel tank with a rubber boot, it is important to remove it now and then to check for rust. The boot makes it more difficult to remove all salt water and it slows drying.

Regulator First Stage

The purpose of the first stage of a regulator is to reduce the pressure from a dive cylinder, providing a constant, stable pressure (intermediate pressure) of air to the second stage, when you inhale.

All first stages are relatively simple mechanical constructions, but there are a couple of principles that are important to know. Common to all regulators is that they are 'fail-safe', which means that if there is a fault in the first stage it does not shut off the air. Instead, the regulator continues supplying air, which generally means it freeflows. So you always get air, as long as there is any left in your cylinder.

The two main types of first stages are piston regulator and membrane regulator. Their purpose and function is the same but the internal mechanisms are different. Each type can be either unbalanced or balanced. Most first stages are balanced today.

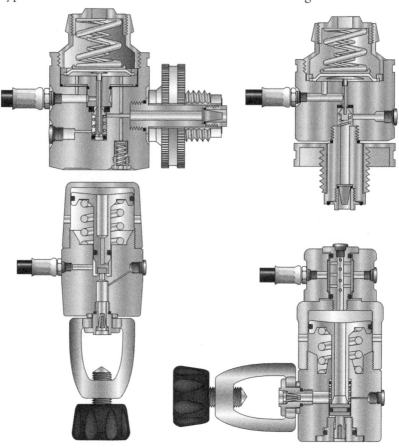

Different functional principles

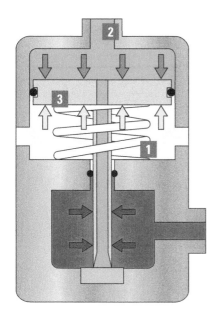

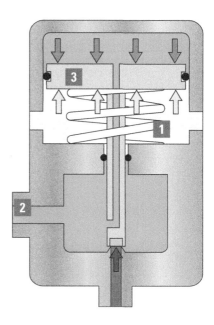

Balanced piston regulator

Tank pressure

In a balanced regulator, the pressure in the cylinder is not an opening force, which means that breathing resistance is unaffected by the pressure in the cylinder. This gives a regulator design that provides greater and more stable airflow compared with an unbalanced design. This is the most common type of piston regulator today. In an unbalanced regulator the pressure in the bottle is an opening *or* closing force, which means that breathing resistance varies with pressure in the cylinder. This presents the designer with challenges that usually result in lower flow than in a balanced regulator.

Intermediate pressure

The pressure in the dive cylinder can vary between 300 bar/4350 psi and almost nothing. In a functional regulator for breathing from, the conditions must be more stable. The purpose of the first stage is to deliver air to the second stage with a pressure of 10 bar/145 psi over the ambient pressure. This is accomplished by the combination of a bias spring and being open so that water can affect intermediate pressure — the higher the water pressure, the higher the intermediate pressure, but always the same amount over the ambient pressure!

Unbalanced piston regulator

Ambient pressure

A regulator adjusted to be easy to breathe on land will be harder to breathe from the deeper you go, if there is no compensation for the increasing pressure. That is the reason why all first stages are open to the surrounding water in some form. Water pressure operates as an opening force on the piston.

Seat

To get a good seal in the opening valve, one of the components is made of a softer material. This is an expendable part that must be replaced regularly. When the regulator is not pressurized, the spring lifts the piston/valve, so the edge doesn't touch the seat. When the regulator is connected to the cylinder and the tank valve is opened, the increase in pressure forces the piston/valve against the seat. This gives the greatest wear and tear to the seat, which can be reduced by slowly opening the valve or by pressing the purge button on the second stage when you open the valve.

1. Bias spring

In a piston regulator, it is this heavy spring that completely determines the intermediate pressure. Normally, there is no opportunity to adjust the spring tension, which means that deviations from the ideal pressure may only be adjusted in the second stage or by inserting thin washers (shims) to increase the intermediate pressure.

2. To second stage

When you start breathing from the second stage, the pressure in the intermediate pressure chamber reduces. Since this is in connection with the space above the piston, the bias spring lifts the piston and air from the cylinder flows to the second stage. When you stop inhaling, the valve in the second stage closes and pressure in the intermediate pressure chamber builds up again until it is large enough to overcame the bias spring tension. The piston is pressed against the seat and closes the airflow.

3. Piston

In a piston first stage, the piston is the only moving part apart from the bias spring. The piston is sealed with two O-rings: one on top; and one at the stem, which can be either in the body or in a groove in the stem. The piston is hollow both in the balanced and unbalanced piston regulators. The difference is that in the balanced regulator, the entire airflow to the second stage goes through the piston. The unbalanced piston regulator uses the channel to equalize the pressure on both sides.

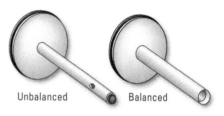

Unbalanced   Balanced

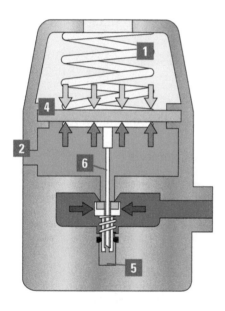

Balanced membrane regulator

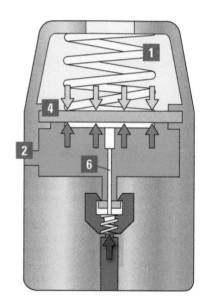

Unbalanced membrane regulator

4. Membrane

The membrane is normally made of silicone and seals the moving parts from the surrounding water. Unlike a piston regulator, there are no O-rings that move in water and the design makes it less prone to freezing in colder water.

5. Balancing chamber

The defining characteristic of a balanced regulator is that the pressure in the dive cylinder is not an opening or closing force. The balancing chamber provides the

same pressure on both sides of the valve (blue) and the high pressure from the cylinder does not affect the movement of the valve.

6. Push rod

The function of the push rod is to transfer the movement of the membrane to the valve.

Balanced piston regulator

Balanced regulators are the most common on the market today. Piston regulators have few parts and are relatively easy to maintain and service. A balanced piston regulator will give, in general, a higher airflow compared with a balanced membrane regulator. However, a piston is more difficult to protect against freezing and is therefore most suitable for diving in water warmer than 8–10°C/46–50°C.

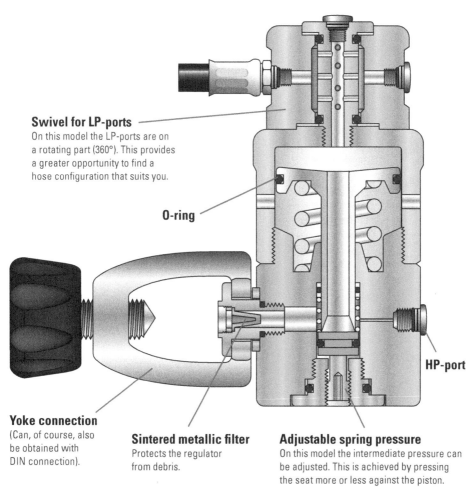

Swivel for LP-ports
On this model the LP-ports are on a rotating part (360°). This provides a greater opportunity to find a hose configuration that suits you.

O-ring

HP-port

Yoke connection
(Can, of course, also be obtained with DIN connection).

Sintered metallic filter
Protects the regulator from debris.

Adjustable spring pressure
On this model the intermediate pressure can be adjusted. This is achieved by pressing the seat more or less against the piston.

Advantages and disadvantages

Piston regulators, both balanced and unbalanced, are robust with few moving parts. The component parts are large and the regulator is relatively easy to service. One weakness is that the piston moves in water, wearing out the O-rings, making it easy to accumulate dirt and deposits in this part. Some designs keep water out while still allowing depth compensation. The design above allows adjustment of the pressure, but this construction is not common. Another way is to unscrew the regulator and put thin washers (shims) between the bias spring and piston, but this means dismantling the regulator and it is therefore not something you should do yourself.

Respiratory cycle: Balanced piston regulator

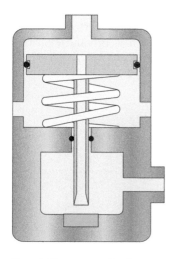

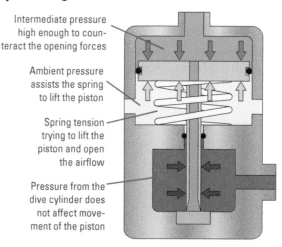

Intermediate pressure high enough to counteract the opening forces

Ambient pressure assists the spring to lift the piston

Spring tension trying to lift the piston and open the airflow

Pressure from the dive cylinder does not affect movement of the piston

Step 1: Not pressurized

Before attaching the regulator or with the tank valve closed, the bias spring lifts the piston from the seat. Ambient pressure in the entire first stage.

Step 2: Pressurized

When you open the tank valve, the first stage is filled with air at higher pressure than the surroundings. Since the valve in the second stage is closed, pressure is built up in the hose and first stage until it is higher than the ambient pressure and bias spring tension. The valve closes.

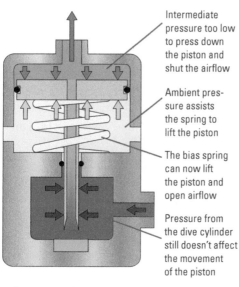

Intermediate pressure too low to press down the piston and shut the airflow

Ambient pressure assists the spring to lift the piston

The bias spring can now lift the piston and open airflow

Pressure from the dive cylinder still doesn't affect the movement of the piston

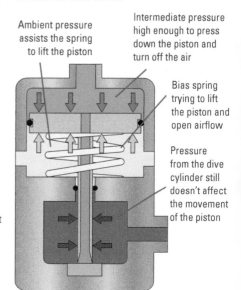

Ambient pressure assists the spring to lift the piston

Intermediate pressure high enough to press down the piston and turn off the air

Bias spring trying to lift the piston and open airflow

Pressure from the dive cylinder still doesn't affect the movement of the piston

Step 3: Inhalation

As shown in *Step 2*, intermediate pressure provides the only closing force and spring tension the only opening force. Ambient pressure assists the spring to lift the piston from the seat, but pressure to the second stage is constant during the entire dive in relation to the ambient pressure. If not so, it would be harder to breathe with increased depth. Inhalation changes the balance of forces—reducing intermediate pressure. The spring, with the help of ambient pressure, can lift the piston and air flows to the second stage.

Step 4: Exhalation

When you stop inhaling, the valve in the second stage closes and pressure is built up in the hose and first stage. Soon the intermediate pressure is high enough to allow the piston to be pushed down and turn off the airflow.

Unbalanced piston regulator

This is a less common design today. Regulators with an unbalanced piston are slightly cheaper and mostly used as rental equipment in warmer climes because they are easy to maintain and service. If you only dive occasionally during holidays to tropical destinations with a divemaster down to 30 metres, this type of regulator is sufficient.

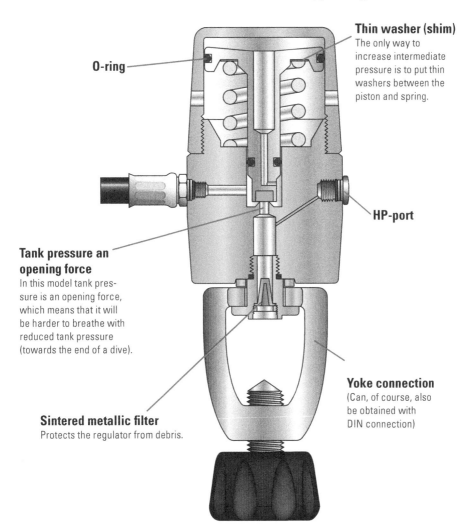

Thin washer (shim)
The only way to increase intermediate pressure is to put thin washers between the piston and spring.

O-ring

HP-port

Tank pressure an opening force
In this model tank pressure is an opening force, which means that it will be harder to breathe with reduced tank pressure (towards the end of a dive).

Yoke connection
(Can, of course, also be obtained with DIN connection)

Sintered metallic filter
Protects the regulator from debris.

Challenges for the designer
The pressure in the cylinder is an opening force in an unbalanced piston regulator, which means that breathing resistance increases with decreasing tank pressure. This design also challenges the engineer when it comes to size. An intermediate pressure of 10 bar/145 psi and a tank pressure of 200 bar/2900 psi means that the surface of the upper part of the piston must be 20 times bigger than the orifice at the sealing surface. Since the airflow is affected by the diameter of the orifice, unbalanced piston regulators normally give less airflow compared to balanced piston regulators.

Respiratory cycle: Unbalanced piston regulator

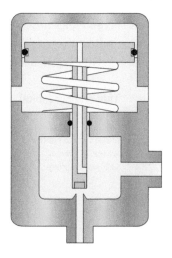

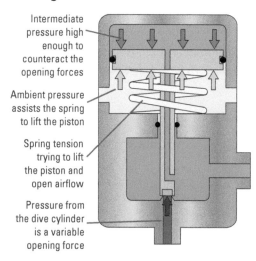

Intermediate pressure high enough to counteract the opening forces

Ambient pressure assists the spring to lift the piston

Spring tension trying to lift the piston and open airflow

Pressure from the dive cylinder is a variable opening force

Step 1: Not pressurized

Before attaching the regulator or with a closed tank valve, the bias spring lifts the piston from the seat. There is ambient pressure in the entire first stage.

Step 2: Pressurized

When the tank valve is opened, the first stage is filled with air at higher pressure than the surroundings. Since the valve in the second stage is closed, pressure is built up in the hose and first stage until it is higher than the ambient pressure and bias spring tension. The valve closes.

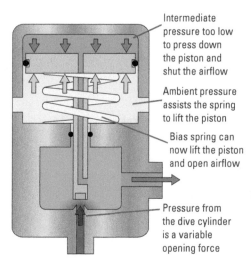

Intermediate pressure too low to press down the piston and shut the airflow

Ambient pressure assists the spring to lift the piston

Bias spring can now lift the piston and open airflow

Pressure from the dive cylinder is a variable opening force

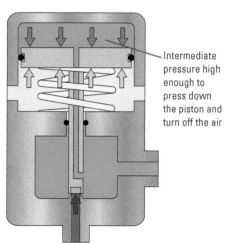

Intermediate pressure high enough to press down the piston and turn off the air

Step 3: Inhalation

Ambient pressure assists the spring to lift the piston from the seat, but the pressure to the second stage is constant during the entire dive in relation to the ambient pressure. If not so, it would be harder to breathe with increased depth.

When you inhale, you change the balance between the forces seen in *Step 2*—inhalation reduces intermediate pressure. The bias spring, with the help of ambient pressure and tank pressure, can lift the piston and air flows to the second stage.

Step 4: Exhalation

When you stop inhaling, the valve in the second stage closes and pressure builds up in the hose and first stage with air from the cylinder. Soon the intermediate pressure is high enough to allow the piston to be pushed down and turn off the airflow.

Balanced membrane regulator

This is a robust construction that works in all environments. Since they have no moving parts in water they are well protected from deposits, dirt and freezing. This is the most common choice for both recreational and technical divers today.

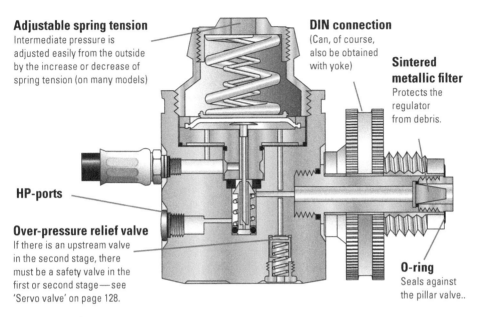

Adjustable spring tension
Intermediate pressure is adjusted easily from the outside by the increase or decrease of spring tension (on many models)

DIN connection
(Can, of course, also be obtained with yoke)

Sintered metallic filter
Protects the regulator from debris.

HP-ports

Over-pressure relief valve
If there is an upstream valve in the second stage, there must be a safety valve in the first or second stage—see 'Servo valve' on page 128.

O-ring
Seals against the pillar valve..

'Over-balanced' membrane regulator

Some manufacturers use the term 'over-balanced' for their first stages. The idea is that the design provides a slightly larger increase in intermediate pressure than ambient pressure alone would give. The argument for this is that air viscosity increases with depth (it becomes more dense), so an over-balanced regulator is more easy-breathing at depth compared to a standard balanced regulator. There are a number of problems with this reasoning:

* At normal recreational diving depths gas viscosity has no importance.
* Most divers use trimix (oxygen, nitrogen, helium) at depths where air viscosity could have significance.
* An increased intermediate pressure gives an increased airflow, but it is the second stage not the first stage that is the limiting part. Most first stages give far more air than the second stage can deliver.
* An over-balanced first stage is normally combined with a balanced second stage. The design of such a second stage means that much of the effect is neutralised. The second stage must be adjustable during the dive to prevent freeflows when the intermediate pressure increases (see page 126).
* 'Over-balanced' as a concept is a bit of a misnomer as it is only the intermediate pressure that is affected.

The design is based on the fact that the bias spring is not open to ambient pressure; instead this area is sealed with an extra membrane. When the pressure increases at depth, the membrane is pushed inwards and affects a piston that helps the bias spring to open the valve. As the extra membrane has a greater surface area than the main membrane, it gives an 'overcompensation' for the ambient pressure, which means that intermediate pressure increases by more than ambient pressure. The extra membrane provides good protection against the environment—freezing, dirt and salt deposits.

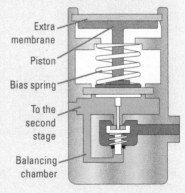

Extra membrane

Piston

Bias spring

To the second stage

Balancing chamber

Respiratory cycle: Balanced membrane regulator

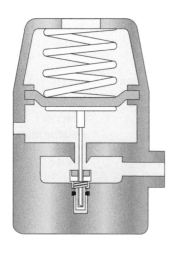

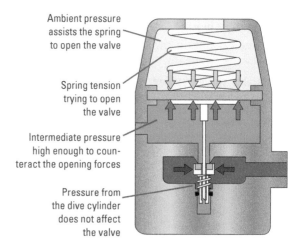

Ambient pressure assists the spring to open the valve

Spring tension trying to open the valve

Intermediate pressure high enough to counteract the opening forces

Pressure from the dive cylinder does not affect the valve

Step 1: Not pressurized

Before attaching the regulator or with the tank valve closed, the bias spring opens the valve. Ambient pressure in the entire first stage.

Step 2: Pressurized

When you open the tank valve, the first stage is filled with air at higher pressure than the surroundings. Since the valve in the second stage is closed, pressure builds up in the hose and first stage until it is higher than the ambient pressure and bias spring tension. The valve closes.

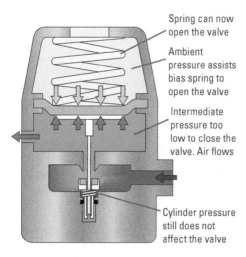

Spring can now open the valve

Ambient pressure assists bias spring to open the valve

Intermediate pressure too low to close the valve. Air flows

Cylinder pressure still does not affect the valve

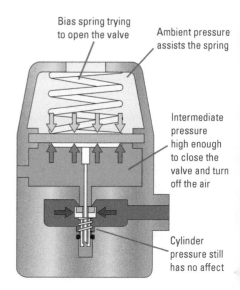

Bias spring trying to open the valve

Ambient pressure assists the spring

Intermediate pressure high enough to close the valve and turn off the air

Cylinder pressure still has no affect

Step 3: Inhalation

Ambient pressure assists the spring to open the valve, but the second stage is constant during the entire dive in relation to the ambient pressure. If not, it would be harder to breathe with increased depth.

Inhalation, changes the balance between the forces seen in *Step 2*—reducing intermediate pressure. The bias spring, with the help of the ambient pressure, can open the valve and air flows to the second stage.

Step 4: Exhalation

When you stop inhaling, the valve in the second stage closes and pressure is built up in the hose and first stage. Soon the intermediate pressure is high enough to allow the valve to be closed and turn off the airflow.

Unbalanced membrane regulator

The first diving regulators were of this design, but now unbalanced membrane regulators are less common. Most membrane regulators that are available on the market are balanced. In this design *tank pressure is a closing force*, which means that it will be *easier* to breathe with reduced tank pressure.

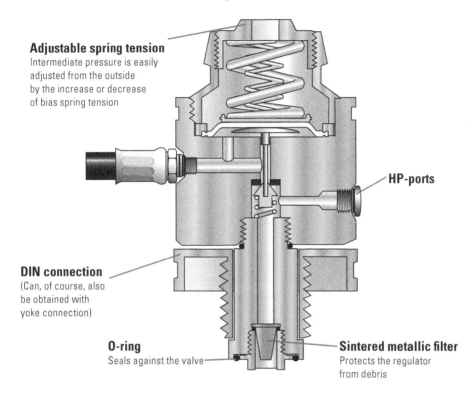

Adjustable spring tension
Intermediate pressure is easily adjusted from the outside by the increase or decrease of bias spring tension

HP-ports

DIN connection
(Can, of course, also be obtained with yoke connection)

O-ring
Seals against the valve

Sintered metallic filter
Protects the regulator from debris

Seat
To get a good seal in the opening valve, one of the components is made of a softer material. In a membrane regulator, this is often located in the valve and is made of a hard plastic material. This is an expendable part that must be replaced regularly. When the regulator is not pressurized, the spring opens the valve. When the regulator is connected to the cylinder and the tank valve is opened, the increase in pressure forces the valve to close. This gives the greatest wear and tear to the seat, which can be reduced by slowly opening the valve or by pressing the purge button on the second stage as you do it.

There are different designs for this valve: 1: The classic high-pressure seat with a mould-in softer part. In 2 and 3, the plastic seal is located in the regulator body. The valve is made of stainless steel and the top is conical or round. This means that there is no sharp edge that works into the seal. Instead, the seat shapes itself to the valve.

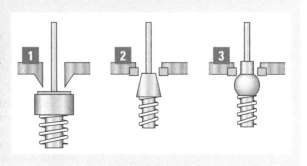

Respiratory cycle: Unbalanced membrane regulator

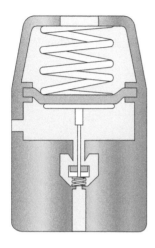

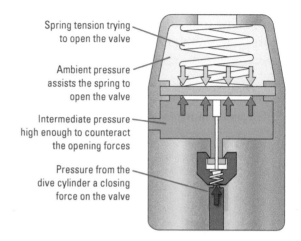

Spring tension trying to open the valve

Ambient pressure assists the spring to open the valve

Intermediate pressure high enough to counteract the opening forces

Pressure from the dive cylinder a closing force on the valve

Step 1: Not pressurized
Before attaching the regulator or with shut tank valve, the bias spring opens the valve. Ambient pressure in the entire first stage.

Step 2: Pressurized
When you open the tank valve, the first stage is filled with air at higher pressure than the surroundings. Since the valve in the second stage is closed, pressure is built up in the hose and first stage until it is higher than the ambient pressure and bias spring tension. The valve closes.

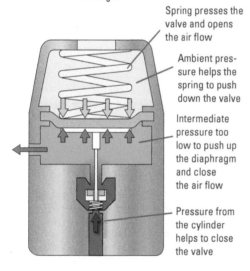

Spring presses the valve and opens the air flow

Ambient pressure helps the spring to push down the valve

Intermediate pressure too low to push up the diaphragm and close the air flow

Pressure from the cylinder helps to close the valve

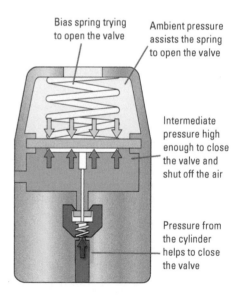

Bias spring trying to open the valve

Ambient pressure assists the spring to open the valve

Intermediate pressure high enough to close the valve and shut off the air

Pressure from the cylinder helps to close the valve

Step 3: Inhalation
As you saw in *Step 2*, the intermediate pressure provides the single closing force and spring tension the only opening. Ambient pressure assists the spring to open the valve, but the pressure in the hose to the second stage is constant in relation to ambient pressure. If not, it would be harder to breathe with increased depth. When you inhale, you change the balance between the forces seen in *Step 2*—inhalation reduces intermediate pressure. The bias spring, with the help of ambient pressure, can open the valve and air flows to the second stage.

Step 4: Exhalation
When you stop inhaling, the valve in the second stage closes and pressure is built up in the hose and first stage. Soon the intermediate pressure is high enough to allow the valve to be closed and turn off the airflow.

Freeze protection

Of all the problems that can occur when diving in cold water, freezing of the first stage is the easiest to avoid. The high pressure from the tank is reduced in the first stage so you get an increase in gas volume. Since the gas molecules are attracted to each other, this means that energy is required to increase the distance between them. This is taken from the kinetic energy of the molecules, so the speed of the molecules will be reduced. We see this as a drop in temperature. This is the same principle as for a common refrigerator. Research has shown that the air temperature very close to the seat in a first stage can be lower than -100°C (-150°F). Of course, this is in a very limited space but it is not uncommon for it to be 5–10° (10–20°F) lower than the surrounding water, so for dives in water colder than 10°C (50°F) regulator freezing is an important consideration. As a first stage is a big chunk of brass, it will be cooled during a dive and if the process goes on long enough ice will be formed on the coldest parts. Modern regulators have a chamber which is open to or is affected by the surrounding water to compensate for the increased ambient pressure at depth. In this chamber is the bias spring (that controls the intermediate pressure). If ice forms here, it disturbs the function of the spring and the valve may get stuck in the open position ('fail-safe'—see page 110) causing a freeflow. This leads to a vicious circle where the flowing air further reduces the temperature and more ice is formed.

The cooling of the first stage during a dive is a fact that we cannot change, but this is really not a problem as long as ice does not form on moving parts. Freeze protection is therefore based on hiding the spring behind a flexible diaphragm and filling the space with a liquid that has a low freezing point. If this is done properly, ice can form on the outside without disturbing the function of the regulator. The problem that can arise is that depth compensation can be lost if ice totally covers the membrane of the compartment containing the anti-freeze-protection.

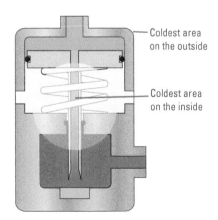

Coldest area on the outside

Coldest area on the inside

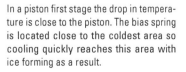

In a piston first stage the drop in temperature is close to the piston. The bias spring is located close to the coldest area so cooling quickly reaches this area with ice forming as a result.

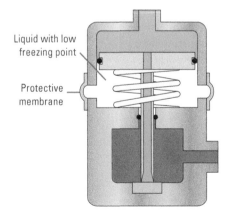

Liquid with low freezing point

Protective membrane

Antifreeze piston regulator
The water inlet holes to the ambient pressure chamber are covered with a flexible membrane and the space around the spring is filled with silicone oil or silicone grease.

A different strategy manufacturers can use is to make the space around the bias spring as open as possible in order to increase water flow and thus prevent icing. Isolating the first stage using plastic only closes the cold in. It is better to make the first stage as large and heavy as possible, but, as usual, this is a compromise with other considerations including weight for travel and cost.

As it is the drop in pressure in the first stage that causes the temperature to decrease, in really cold water it is better to dive with a 200–232 bar/2900–3300 psi cylinder compared to one of 300 bar/4350 psi. The risk of freezing is also greater at the beginning of a dive with a full cylinder as there is a bigger pressure drop.

As the air inside the regulator can help create ice formation, if we fill our tanks from a badly maintained compressor, any water vapour present in the air can form ice crystals inside the system. This is uncommon, but it gives you one more reason to demand quality fills from your local dive shop. Ice can also, of course, form in the second stage—see 'Second stage freezing' on page 130.

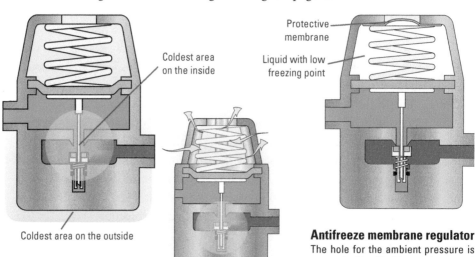

Protective membrane

Coldest area on the inside

Liquid with low freezing point

Coldest area on the outside

The temperature drop is far from the moving parts. The push rod is on the other side of the membrane so it takes a long time for this area to cool.

A well-designed membrane regulator with no anti-freeze protection can have ice on the bottom but still operate, particularly if there are vents around the bias spring for water circulation. It usually needs no additional anti-freeze protection.

Antifreeze membrane regulator
The hole for the ambient pressure is covered with a flexible membrane and the space around the bias spring is filled with silicone oil or silicone grease.

Summary

You now have a good understanding of how the different types of first stages work. The key is to see how the various forces act on the moving parts—what the different opening and closing forces are.

After the section on second stages, we will look at the various designs and the considerations that are important when choosing a regulator.

Regulator Second Stage

It requires training, proper tools, access to spare parts and manufacturers' model-specific manuals to service regulators. The purpose of this section is for you to understand the way different types of regulators function. It is not a replacement for a service and repair course.

The intermediate pressure delivered from the first stage must be further reduced to produce a gas you are able to breathe. This is done in the second stage, giving you gas with the same pressure as the surrounding water. The second stage will only give you gas when you inhale, it is otherwise closed. This type of valve is called a demand valve.

Inhalation

Inhalation makes the diaphragm bulge inwards and press the lever, which opens the valve. The second stage housing is open to the surrounding water to compensate for the depth. It provides gas at the ambient pressure.

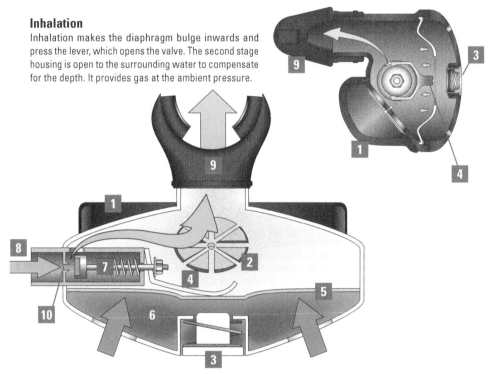

1. Exhaust tee

Most regulators today have bottom exhausts. These allow exhaust gas to be evenly distributed on the sides of the head when looking straight ahead. Tilt the head and the gas takes the easiest route up. See page 128 for examples with side exhausts.

2. Exhaust valve

Usually a thin silicone membrane that only opens in one direction. If you get water in the regulator when you inhale it is likely that dirt is impairing a good seal. The membrane could also be damaged and need to be replaced.

3. Purge button

An important feature for clearing water. Make sure that you can manage it with the gloves you will wear.

4. Lever

Transfers the diaphragm movements to the valve. Design varies, but the function remains the same.

5. Diaphragm

When you inhale, the drop in pressure makes the diaphragm bulge in. The inward movement pushes the lever and opens the valve. You probably realize that it is imperative that this diaphragm remains completely intact, otherwise the second stage will not work as intended. But it is well protected under the cover so problems are rare.

6. Ambient pressure

To compensate for ambient pressure, the diaphragm must be in contact with the surrounding water. It also keeps water out of the part where the air flows.

7. Valve
Most modern second stages are based on a downstream valve. The intermediate pressure opens the valve, but to balance this the spring is just strong enough to close it again. The spring tension can be adjusted with a nut on the end of the valve assembly.

8. Air from the first stage
Air is delivered at as constant pressure as possible — normally around 10 bar/145 psi above ambient pressure (see page 111). Some second stages can have the hose routed from left or right — so you can change your configuration to suit. This could be useful for an alternative air source (see page 131).

9. Mouthpiece
Second stages come with a standard mouthpiece. Even if the manufacturer has done their best to find a form that is suitable for most divers, you may not find it comfortable. Mouthpieces in other shapes, sizes and colours are sold as accessories, so there is a good chance that you will find one that suits you. When you do, get an extra one for your 'save-a-dive' kit.

10. Orifice
The orifice must be large enough to provide sufficient air and small enough to give a low breathing resistance, so this is a delicate compromise for engineers. There are a number of ways to handle this, which are described on the following pages.

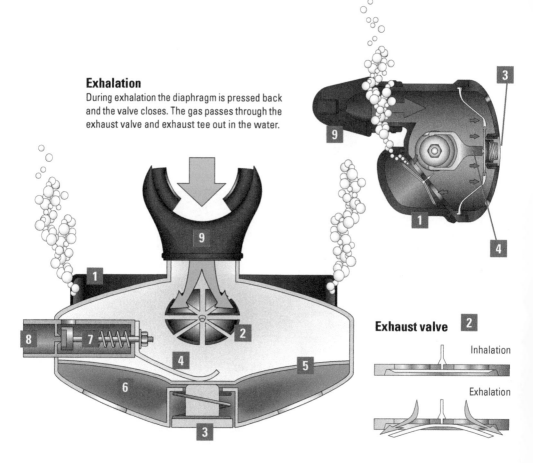

Exhalation
During exhalation the diaphragm is pressed back and the valve closes. The gas passes through the exhaust valve and exhaust tee out in the water.

Exhaust valve [2]

Inhalation

Exhalation

A key objective of second stage design is to minimize breathing resistance and there are different strategies for this — just as there are with first stages. There are both balanced and unbalanced models. Instead of a downstream valve, some models are based on a servo valve, which helps to open the larger main valve. The air you exhale can be distributed evenly on both sides of your head or only on one side. The inside of the second stage can employ different methods to ensure that the flowing air holds the valve open during inhalation.

Downstream or upstream

Most modern second stages have a downstream valve. This means that the pressure from the first stage helps to open the valve, but to balance this pressure requires a spring that is slightly stronger. For this there is usually a set screw to increase or decrease the spring tension.

The problem with the design is that it assumes that the first stage delivers constant pressure to the second stage. Variations result in either increased or decreased breathing resistance or a freeflow. The ability to freeflow due to increased intermediate pressure is an important safety function called *fail-safe*, which ensures that air flows as long as there is some left in the cylinder.

Downstream valve

In this design intermediate pressure from the first stage is cancelled out by spring tension. When the diver inhales, the valve is opened by the lever.

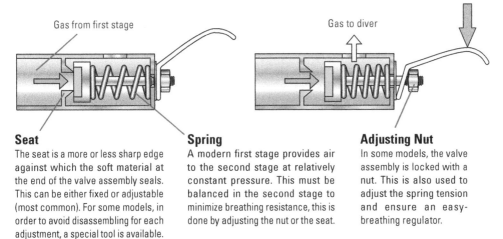

Gas from first stage

Gas to diver

Seat
The seat is a more or less sharp edge against which the soft material at the end of the valve assembly seals. This can be either fixed or adjustable (most common). For some models, in order to avoid disassembling for each adjustment, a special tool is available.

Spring
A modern first stage provides air to the second stage at relatively constant pressure. This must be balanced in the second stage to minimize breathing resistance, this is done by adjusting the nut or the seat.

Adjusting Nut
In some models, the valve assembly is locked with a nut. This is also used to adjust the spring tension and ensure an easy-breathing regulator.

Upstream valve

In an upstream valve, inhalation causes the diaphragm to press a rocker (right-hand arrow):

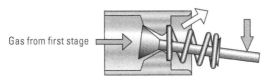

Gas from first stage

It is of a simple design and the spring-loaded rocker gives very easy breathing, but it must be combined with a *pressure relief valve* (see page 129) to be fail-safe.

Balanced or unbalanced

Just as with first stages, second stages can be unbalanced or balanced and the design is based on the same principles—a balanced valve should be unaffected by the pressure coming from the first stage.

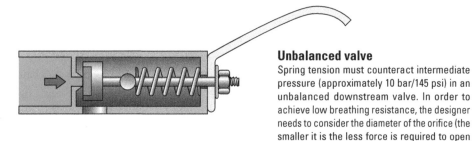

Unbalanced valve
Spring tension must counteract intermediate pressure (approximately 10 bar/145 psi) in an unbalanced downstream valve. In order to achieve low breathing resistance, the designer needs to consider the diameter of the orifice (the smaller it is the less force is required to open the valve) and the design of the lever.

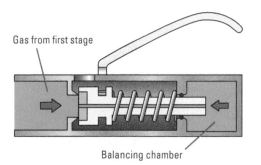

Gas from first stage

Balancing chamber

Balanced valve
In this type of second stage the valve moves in approximately the same pressure on both sides, meaning the spring can be made considerably weaker. The diver uses much less force to open the valve.

The valve is hollow so air from the first stage can enter the balancing chamber on the other side of the valve. Intermediate pressure is an opening force, but the opposite force from the balancing chamber and the spring perfectly counters it. Intermediate pressure therefore acts to enable both opening and closing, and the orifice in the valve can be made larger and thus give a greater airflow without increasing breathing resistance.

In a balanced valve, the pressure is the same on both sides. The surface of the orifice of the valve provides an opening force, while the surface on the back of the valve together with the spring tension provides the closing force. This is the same principle as balanced and unbalanced valves in first stages.

Adjustable breathing resistance

Some second stages have a knob on the outside to make it possible to adjust the breathing resistance during a dive to adapt to depth, activity, workload, increased water flow when diving in a current, etc. The illustration on page 127 shows a second stage with a balanced valve and adjustable breathing resistance. This is a fairly common design, sometimes also supplemented with a Venturi control.

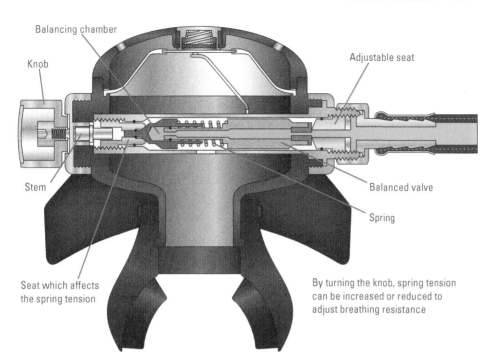

Balancing chamber

Knob

Adjustable seat

Stem

Balanced valve

Spring

Seat which affects
the spring tension

By turning the knob, spring tension
can be increased or reduced to
adjust breathing resistance

Venturi effect

Engineers also work with the flow inside the second stage
housing. They want the flowing gas to create a negative
pressure on the inside of the diaphragm so that the lever is
held down as long as you inhale. This is called the Venturi
effect. On some second stages it can be adjusted in-dive.

If a second stage is designed
without regard to the Venturi
effect, the flow inside the
housing will be uncontrolled

Flowing air directed to cause negative pressure
on the inside of the diaphragm.

In this model, a knob/
lever controls the
position of the flap (in
red) which adjusts the
airflow in the housing

Some second stages have
a plastic sleeve around
the valve assembly,
which makes it possible
to adjust the direc-
tion of the out-flowing
air so as to affect the
breathing resistance.

Full Venturi—decreased
breathing resistance

Air directed against the
diaphragm—increased resistance

Side exhaust

Most modern second stages have exhausts on both sides—bottom exhaust. However, there are advantages to having the exhaust on just one side: there is no 'correct' way around, you have freedom to arrange it to come in from the right or left, as you prefer. This is a clear advantage for an extra second stage in a stressful emergency situation.

With a standard regulator, external pressure on the diaphragm can become so great that the valve opens unintentionally, for example if you swim against strong currents or use an underwater scooter. With the diaphragm on the side, this does not happen. The side exhaust style is usually also better at keeping bubbles away from your face when you look straight ahead, an advantage for underwater photographers.

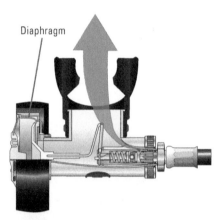

Diaphragm

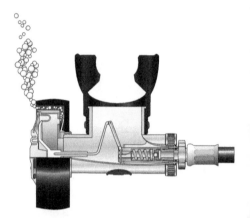

This example second stage operates by the same principles as bottom exhaust models. When the diver inhales, the diaphragm bulges in and opens the valve via the lever.

On exhalation, the diaphragm is pushed back and the lever closes the valve. The exhaust valve opens to release air.

Servo valve

Most modern cars have power steering to reduce the energy needed to perform what used to be strenuous work. Similarly, some modern second stages have a servo valve to avoid some problems connected to using a downstream valve. This design allows bigger orifices to be used, thereby giving higher flow without increasing breathing resistance. The second stage is also less sensitive to variations in intermediate pressure.

Most servo valves have an upstream design. This means that intermediate pressure is a closing force. During your entry-level course, you practiced how to breathe from a freeflowing regulator. An upstream valve doesn't freeflow in the event of a first stage malfunction. With an upstream valve you don't need to use any special technique—you just breathe normally from the regulator on the way to the surface. To make this design fail-safe, excess air is released through a pressure relief valve which is installed either in the first stage or the second stage.

When you inhale, the bulging diaphragm affects the valve and opens it. The difference from a downstream valve is that the valve don't seal against a sharp edge, so the sealing surface is more durable.

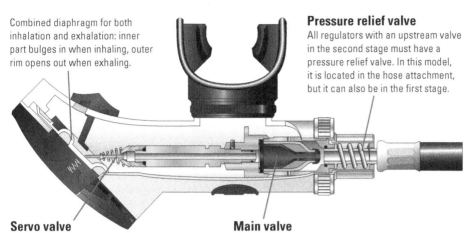

Combined diaphragm for both inhalation and exhalation: inner part bulges in when inhaling, outer rim opens out when exhaling.

Pressure relief valve

All regulators with an upstream valve in the second stage must have a pressure relief valve. In this model, it is located in the hose attachment, but it can also be in the first stage.

Servo valve

This is a small valve that doesn't require a lot of force to stay closed and therefore not much force to be opened.

Main valve

The small servo valve opens with little effort. The air that flows through the main valve opens it. This design gives a large and stable airflow with little effort.

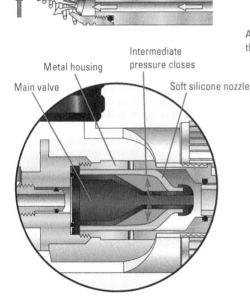

Main valve

Metal housing

Intermediate pressure closes

Soft silicone nozzle

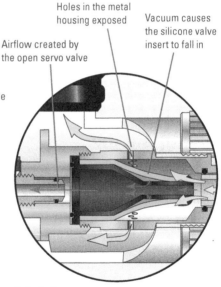

Holes in the metal housing exposed

Vacuum causes the silicone valve insert to fall in

Airflow created by the open servo valve

Exhalation/no breathing

When you exhale or when the regulator is pressurized but not used, the intermediate pressure forces the soft silicone valve insert to be pressed against the holes in the metal housing. No air can escape.

Inhalation

On inhalation, the small servo valve opens and air flows through the main valve. The soft walls are sucked in and uncover holes in the metal housing. The total area of these holes is much larger than what can be achieved with a standard downstream valve, which gives a greater airflow.

Either or

Some divers feel that second stages with servo valves 'flutter' on inhalation, especially at shallower depths. This is due to the small delay between the opening of the servo valve and the main valve. With the correct breathing technique—inhaling slowly, not gasping—this problem disappears. But divers seem to be divided into two camps: those who like this type of regulator and those who don't. But it is an educated guess that few have actually tried a servo valve!

Second stage freezing

We discussed freezing in the first stage earlier (on page 121), but you also face the risk of this happening in the second stage while diving in cold water. As the reduction in pressure is considerably smaller, the risk is much lower than in the first stage. The biggest problem is instead moisture from exhalation, especially if the air temperature is low enough. The water vapour you exhale when we test the regulator before the dive can be enough to freeze the valve stuck in the open position. In such conditions, it is better to wait to breathe from the regulator until it is totally submerged and to keep it below the surface until the dive is finished.

Some manufacturers have special second stages adapted for cold water diving. These designs make it difficult for the ice to form on metal parts and/or direct the exhaled air to warm parts where ice should not form. Some have metal parts with flanges to serve as heat sinks.

There are also regulators on the market that are totally unsuitable for diving in cold water or even impossible to retrofit with freeze protection. So make sure that you use one that is made for cold water diving or is possible to freeze protect if you intend to dive in water colder than 8–10°C (46–50° F). If you plan on buying equipment while on holiday in a tropical destination, this is an important consideration. But it does not only apply to winter diving—at higher latitudes in the summer at depths of 30–40 m/100–130 ft temperatures can be low enough to cause freezing in an unsuitable regulator.

Buying advice

Consider first what kind of diving you will be doing: will you be diving in cold water, so need freeze-protection? Are you likely only to dive on holiday? What type of tank connector is common where you do most diving? Will you need space on your first stage for a drysuit hose?

Buying a regulator is about the same as buying a car: there are no really bad products on the market, you get what you pay for and performance can deteriorate quickly with absent or incorrect care, maintenance and service. This means that one of the most important factors is that you can have it serviced in the area where you live. So a visit to your local dive centre is a good start. It is also possible to have servicing done by mail order in some places, although this will incur additional cost and risk—make sure your package is well-padded and insured.

It is most convenient to buy a set (of first and second stage) of the same brand. This way you can be certain that they fit together and not all manufacturers use the same intermediate pressure.

Budget is, of course, a consideration. But invest as much as you can in your regulator and instead save on gadgets that don't have equal importance. Your regulator may be the most expensive item in your kit but with care it may also last the longest.

Alternate Air Source

All divers probably agree that the most serious incident that can occur underwater is an out-of-air situation. There are two different ways to solve this problem — with the help of your buddy and with a fully independent gas system.

With the help of your buddy

The most common solution is to use your buddy for help and this is also the preferred way taught by most diving education agencies. An extra second stage (octopus) is the most accepted alternate air source internationally and most divers see it as a compulsory part of their diving equipment. Extra second stages work the same way as the normal second stage, but the hose is usually about 20 cm/8 in longer to facilitate a buddy using it during the ascent. You will find many opinions about how the extra second stage should be used, but most divers prefer that the diver without air grab it. A common mistake is to try to use it upside-down, so many divers choose a model where this doesn't matter.

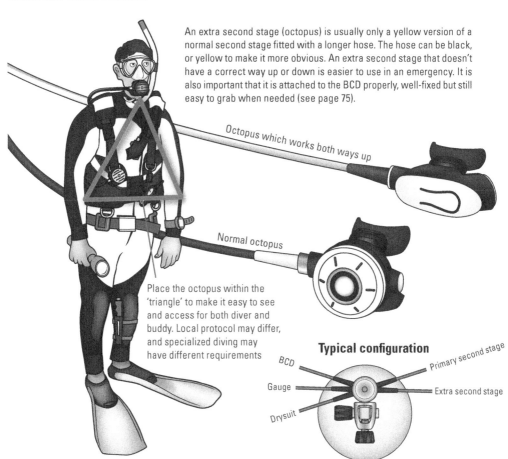

An extra second stage (octopus) is usually only a yellow version of a normal second stage fitted with a longer hose. The hose can be black, or yellow to make it more obvious. An extra second stage that doesn't have a correct way up or down is easier to use in an emergency. It is also important that it is attached to the BCD properly, well-fixed but still easy to grab when needed (see page 75).

Octopus which works both ways up

Normal octopus

Place the octopus within the 'triangle' to make it easy to see and access for both diver and buddy. Local protocol may differ, and specialized diving may have different requirements

Typical configuration

BCD

Gauge

Drysuit

Primary second stage

Extra second stage

To avoid one hose, some manufacturers have combined an inflator with an alternate air source. You must have a hose for the inflator anyway, so this seems like a good solution. However, the disadvantage is that the donor must give away his or her primary second stage and then breathe from the inflator-regulator. For this reason, the hose to the normal second stage should be extra long, but few recreational divers have this since it is rather cumbersome to swim around with a long hose sticking out on the side.

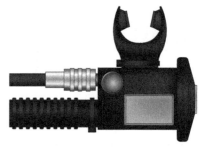

Inflator that also works as an extra second stage

Self-help

Both the above solutions assume that you have a buddy nearby to help you out. A totally independent ('redundant') air supply allows you to solve an out of air emergency without the aid of another diver. It reduces the risk of misunderstanding and solves the problems of separation or the buddy's extra second stage malfunctioning.

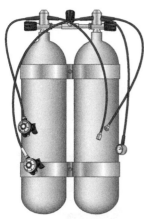

Twin tanks
There are many ways to configure a twinset for independent diving, both in terms of hose location and distribution between the two first stages. The location also affects the length of the hoses. A typical set-up:

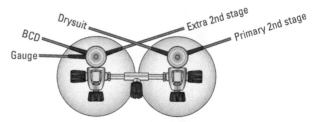

In technical diving, a 210 cm/7 ft long hose is often used on the primary second stage. If you need to share gas with a diver in distress, they take the primary second stage and you use the extra second stage yourself, which is often located in a rubber necklace.

Y-valve/H-valve
A typical set up for diving with a Y-valve on a single tank. Of course, there are other ways to configure this, both when it comes to hose location and distribution between the two regulators.

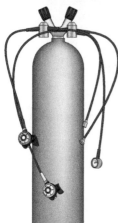

Twin tanks (twinsets) with separate regulators are a long-used method. As you saw in the section on cylinders (see page 106), there are other ways to configure them. This arrangement also works for a single cylinder, but then you do not have true redundancy. You must have a pillar valve with two separate regulator connections, i.e. a Y-valve, which lets you have two independent regulator systems. If one begins to freeflow, you shut that valve off and continue to breathe from the other regulator.

A truly independent system requires two first stages with at least one second stage attached to each. This solution is not unusual among divers exploring places where there is no direct access to the surface, for example, in cave diving and wreck diving.

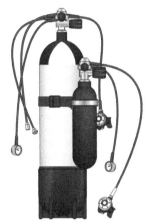

Pony bottle

The configuration for a pony-bottle depends to some extent if you choose to put it on the right or left-hand side of the dive cylinder. This is a typical set up but many divers still have two second stages on their main cylinder, and there are other ways to place and distribute the hoses between the two first stages. The location also determines the length of the hoses.

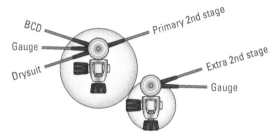

A simple solution is a pony-bottle. This is a small tank with a separate regulator that is usually clamped to the main tank. Should your main regulator freeze or malfunction, you just switch to your independent air supply and make an ascent. There are both 200/232 bar (2900/3300 psi) and 300 bar (4350 psi) cylinders and depending on size they offer around 500 to 900 litres/18 to 32 cu.ft of air. This should be enough to get you to the surface on non-decompression dives, including a safety stop.

Some divers see a SpareAir as an independent supply, but its use is limited due to the small volume of air it holds. It has a built-in regulator and is supplied with a filling adapter so you can fill it from your normal tank. Spare Air gives about 80 litres/2.8 cu ft of air and although this might be sufficient in some cases to take you to the surface, there will probably not be enough air for a safety stop or room for error.

Independence

Our training bodies teach us that in the case of an emergency we should just get the attention of our buddy and everything will be solved as long as we follow our training. Solo diving is rarely talked about since it is forbidden ground. While the educational organizations still hold to that idea, they also accept the fact that there is a place for solo divers. Many have introduced courses to improve diver independence. One of the requirements is an independent air supply. If all divers planned their dives as independent dives many incidents and emergencies could be avoided. An independent air system is therefore a good investment.

Regulators — Summary

With two different connections to the tank valve, four main types of first stages and three basic models of second stages, it is not an easy task to choose the right regulator.

Downstream with bottom exhaust

The most common type of second stage. Its downstream valve is a simple design, which can be complemented with a balanced valve, adjustable Venturi and adjustable breathing resistance. Exhausts on both sides distribute the bubbles well during normal forward swimming. There is a large range so compare: breathing resistance; airflow; balanced or unbalanced valve; adjustable Venturi; weight; and fit of the mouthpiece.

Side exhaust

This is essentially the same design as the bottom exhaust, but the diaphragm is turned 90 degrees. Side exhaust second stages have many missionaries because they often have high performance and are easy to use. There is no up or down, right-hand or left-hand so it does not matter how you insert it in your mouth. This is an important safety feature in case of an emergency. They also offer greater configuration opportunities. Many underwater photographers prefer this type of regulator because they are better at keeping bubbles away from your face when you look straight ahead. The range is limited — there are not many models to choose from and most are designed as alternate second stages (octopus).

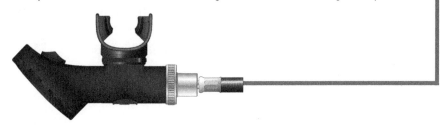

Servo valve

These second stages provide great performance but not all divers like them. Some people think that they give too much air, or a sense that air is being pushed into the mouth. You must breathe slowly and not gasp. This is a robust second stage with top performance regarding low breathing resistance and large airflow. Second stages with a servo valve also have the reputation of being sensitive and complex to maintain, but it is actually the contrary, these regulators have fewer moving parts and they are insensitive to normal variations in intermediate pressure. The range is limited, with only a few models and manufacturers to choose from.

Balanced piston

A common modern regulator. They have few parts and are relatively easy to maintain and service. A balanced piston regulator gives, in general, a higher airflow compared with a balanced membrane regulator but this difference is of little importance — see 'Balanced membrane' below. Piston regulators are more difficult to protect against freezing than membrane regulators, so are more suitable for diving in water warmer than 8–10°C/40–50°F.

Unbalanced piston

Slightly cheaper and most are used as rental equipment in warmer places because they are easy to maintain and service. Modern designs, however, do not give significantly large variations in breathing resistance. If you only dive in tropical climes, this is still a good choice.

Balanced membrane

A robust design that works in all environments. Since there are no moving parts exposed to water, they are well protected from salt deposits, dirt and freezing. This is the most common choice among recreational divers. Membrane regulators can normally be made smaller and lighter than piston regulators, which makes them a good choice if you travel a lot and want to pack as light as possible. The flow from a membrane regulator is often less than a corresponding piston regulator, but it is the second stage that is the limiting part, so the difference is of little importance.

Unbalanced membrane

The first regulators made for diving were this type, but they are now less common. Most modern membrane regulators are balanced. Modern unbalanced ones are, however, robust, and they do not give significantly large variations in breathing resistance, so for holiday diving this can be a good choice. Unbalanced membrane first stages can also be a good choice for special purposes, like stage kits and drysuit cylinders (see page 182).

Yoke (A-clamp)

Internationally, the most common connection to the tank valve. The yoke is placed over the valve and the sealing O-ring is seated in the valve. Only approved for pressures up to 232 bar/3300 psi.

If you intend to buy a regulator and only use it for holiday diving trips where you rent a cylinder the choice is simple — a yoke connector. If you want your own cylinders, the choice is a little trickier. Then you need to consider what type of cylinder you want — 200/232 bar (2900/3300 psi) or 300 bar (4350 psi) and select the regulator accordingly.

Many technical divers use DIN connection regardless of which cylinders they have as the O-ring is better protected, reducing the risk of problems.

DIN

Common in Europe and available in two main versions — for 200 bar/2900 psi and for 300 bar/4350 psi pillar valves. The only difference between the two is the number of threads in order to avoid confusing regulators made for different pressure ratings. Virtually all regulators with DIN connection now have the one for 300 bar/4350 psi. With an adapter, can be used on valves that only allow yoke connections. So you have no limitations.

There is a third version used to distinguish regulators intended for diving with a higher fraction of oxygen than air (nitrox). This connection has a larger M26 diameter so will not fit in a standard pillar valve.

How good are modern regulators?

Even if you consider that diving regulators are fairly simple mechanical designs, there is a huge difference between modern regulators and the double-hose invention that Cousteau began to dive with. Few modern divers, consider an airflow of 140 litres per minute/5 cu ft per minute as sufficient (second stages now give up to 2000 litres per minute/70 cu ft per minute, although that is during freeflow) and breathing resistance today is close to negligible — we don't have to suck air from the cylinder.

The evolution of diving regulators has been a continuous process parallel with general technical development regarding design, manufacturing techniques and new materials. There are three crucial events considered as giant leaps for this development:

The US Navy tests

In scuba diving's infancy, regulators were tested by diving with them — if they supplied air during the entire dive the performance was considered good. When the US Navy began formal tests, it put pressure on manufacturers to develop their products. Being on the US Navy list of approved regulators was a marketable quality. However, it is important to recognize that the US Navy had no involvement in the development of the technology, they just checked out which models met their criteria for military diving.

The ANSTI breathing simulator

In the early 1990s, some highly-skilled engineers at the company ANSTI in England created a breathing simulator that in a precise and controlled manner could test regulator performance. The ANSTI machine quickly became the industry standard and there is no regulator manufacturer that can do without it today. The ANSTI machine simulates breathing under different conditions and the sensors are connected to a computer that analyses raw data and displays the results as text and graphics.

The ANSTI-Chart shows the breathing resistance of a regulator, both inhalation and exhalation. It should be read clockwise from the starting point — it starts with inhalation and ends with exhalation. The graph shows a few different cases to illustrate some typical performances. See page 137 for an example and explanation.

EN 250

In 2000, the EU agreed on a common European standard for diving apparatuses — *EN 250:2000: Respiratory equipment. Open-circuit self-contained compressed air diving apparatus. Requirements, testing, marking.* This gave producers a detailed description of how a scuba regulator must be able to perform in order to be approved for sale in the EU. It is not only manufacturers in EU countries that are interested in meeting these requirements, EN 250:2000 has set a worldwide standard and been incorporated in national standards outside the EU. EN 250:2000 was replaced in April 2014 by EN 250:2014.

The requirements of EN 250:

Breathing rate:
25 breaths per minute (bpm).

Tidal volume: 2.5 litres.
(Volume in a normal breath).

This gives:
Ventilation Rate: 62.5 litres per minute (Respiratory Minute Volume, RMV). This is very high. Normal breathing is assumed to be about 25 litres per minute, so test conditions are 2.5 times higher.

Inhale Pressure: Max -25 mbar.

Inhale Positive Pressure: Max +5 mbar — Venturi must not be so substantial as to prevent air being pushed into the mouth.

Exhale Pressure: max +25 mbar.

Ext Work of Breathing (WOB):
Max 3 J / l. The sum of the following. The figure is quite high and easily achieved by modern regulators.

Inhale Work: The work required to inhale. The unit is Joule per litre (J / l).

Pos Inhale Work: Max 0.3 J / l. Again, Venturi is good but it must not be so substantial that it works to prevent air being pushed into the mouth.

Exhale Work: The work that is required to exhale air in the water. There is little performance different between modern regulators.

The example shows a regulator that can easily handle EN 250

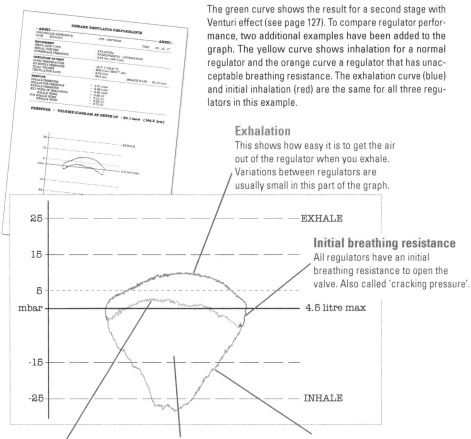

The green curve shows the result for a second stage with Venturi effect (see page 127). To compare regulator performance, two additional examples have been added to the graph. The yellow curve shows inhalation for a normal regulator and the orange curve a regulator that has unacceptable breathing resistance. The exhalation curve (blue) and initial inhalation (red) are the same for all three regulators in this example.

Exhalation
This shows how easy it is to get the air out of the regulator when you exhale. Variations between regulators are usually small in this part of the graph.

Initial breathing resistance
All regulators have an initial breathing resistance to open the valve. Also called 'cracking pressure'.

4.5 litre max

Significant Venturi
Once the valve opens, the Venturi effect takes over and presses the air into the divers mouth. This positive pressure may not exceed 5 mbar.

An approved regulator
This curve shows a relatively easy breathing regulator without significant Venturi effect.

A failed regulator
This regulator is not approved according to EN 250. The breathing resistance is too great.

Preparation

A new regulator requires some care. If you buy a complete set with extra second stage and pressure gauge/console, you should ask to have it assembled in the store. The fittings in a modern first stage are sized to make it impossible to confuse hoses for high pressure and low pressure, but store staff will know where to place the various hoses for the best comfort and function (and see page 131).

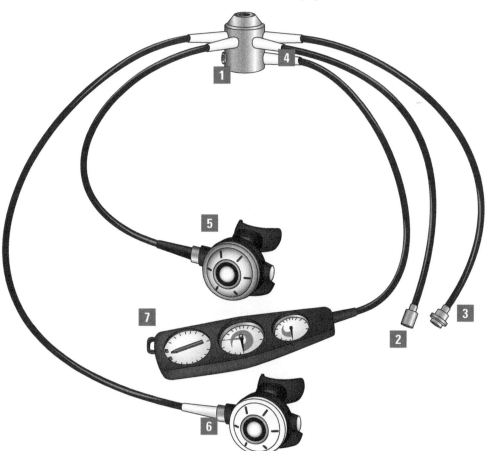

1. Regulator first stage

First stages are equipped with a number of ports for both low pressure (LP, second stage and inflator hose) and high pressure (HP, pressure gauge). Some first stages, have a special output for the primary second stage with greater airflow than the other low-pressure outputs.

2. Low-pressure hose for the BCD

This hose is included when you buy a BCD. Most manufacturers use the same international standard, so you do not normally need to replace it if you change BCD. The inflator hose is normally routed over your left shoulder.

3. Low-pressure hose for the drysuit

This hose is included when you buy a drysuit. There are a few different fittings on the market and they are not interchangeable. This hose is normally routed via your left side.

4. Hose protectors

All hoses can be fitted with a hose protector to reduce wear. Hose protectors are available in different designs and colours, so it is also a way to make your regulator more personal. The hoses must be removed from the first stage for you to be able fit the hose protectors. They slide on easier if they are first put in hot water for a few minutes beforehand.

5. Regulator second stage

Normally you buy the first stage and second stage in a package, this way you can be sure that they will work well together. If you buy them separately, it is important to ensure that they have characteristics and performance that are compatible. The intermediate pressure delivered by the first stage must be the same as the second stage was made for, but with an adjustable second stage there is some flexibility. With an upstream second stage, there must be an over-pressure relief valve in the first stage or in the hose connection. Some first stages have a special port for the primary second stage to give a greater airflow. This is clearly marked.

6. Alternative air source

If you choose an extra second stage as an alternate air source (rather than an independent air source), the standard position is for the hose to be on the right side, and come over the shoulder or under the arm. See 'Alternate Air Source' on page 131 onwards for more on configurations.

7. Instruments/dive computer

This can mean everything from a traditional pressure gauge to a transmitter that is attached to the first stage and sends information wirelessly to a dive computer on your wrist.

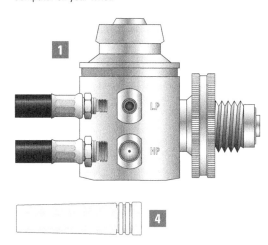

Care and maintenance

A regulator is the only item of your diving equipment that you should never disassemble yourself. They are simple mechanical constructions, but without training and proper tools it is easy to turn them into dangerous devices. If you want to change configuration or add something (e.g. a drysuit hose), it is important to use the right tools and to put the hose(s) in the right place. To avoid mix-ups, all manufacturers use different sized threads for the connections to the high-pressure and low-pressure ports.

A good way to keep an eye on how the regulator is doing is to use an intermediate pressure gauge. This is an accurate pressure gauge that measures up to 20 bar/300 psi and that connects to the inflator hose. Measuring the intermediate pressure is like a doctor using a stethoscope to check your breathing and heart. Intermediate pressure should be approximately 10 bar/145 psi and it should fall quickly when you inhale and return quickly when you exhale. It should also stay constant when you do not breathe. Most membrane regulators allow you to adjust the intermediate pressure if it is too high or too low. Turning the ring that holds it in place adjusts the tension of the bias spring (see page 117).

Any work on the regulator beyond these items should be handed over to a trained professional. To do a complete regulator service, you need special training and authorisation from the manufacturer/distributor. Summaries of incident reports clearly show that if all divers followed the recommendations for an annual service, a large portion of the problems with regulators would disappear. Therefore, take care of your regulator and to ensure it achieves the expected performance hand it in for service at regular intervals—just as you do with your car. Unlike a car, the amount of use has little influence on the need for servicing. If you frequently use your regulator there may be some wear on the O-rings, however, O-rings that are not subject to use will lose their flexibility. To realize the importance of regular servicing, you must understand how a regulator works (see page 110 onwards). Some regulator manufacturers offer a lifetime warranty covering parts, however the warranty is void if you miss an annual service.

Protecting the first stage

The seal between the cylinder valve and the regulator is important. For a yoke regulator the O-ring is in the cylinder valve and is easy to inspect before screwing on the regulator. With DIN, the O-ring is seated in the regulator. Make sure it is in place and that it is intact before every dive. Store regulators with their caps on.

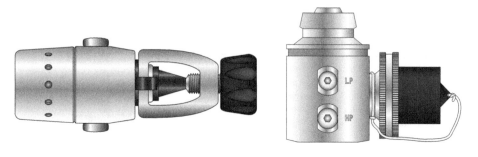

1. Valve in the second stage

Most second stages have a downstream valve, which means that they open if the pressure becomes greater than a set value. If there is any fault on the first stage, for example, if ice is forming in the ambient pressure chamber, the second stage will freeflow.

In normal diving, you want the regulator to be as easy breathing as possible, which means that the second stage valve should be set against intermediate pressure so that it opens with the least possible effort. If only small adjustments are necessary, this can be done on both an adjustable first stage and second stage.

2. To alternate air source

There are different types of alternate air source, so not all divers have this configuration (see page 131).

3. Hex (Allen) key

By turning the ring, you increase or decrease the tension on the bias spring. If the valve in the second stage leaks, you reduce the tension and if it is hard breathing you increase the tension. This is possible to do on most membrane first stages, but few piston first stages. Please note that problems with the second stage can be caused by things other than the intermediate pressure, like dirt or a worn seat.

4. Bias spring

It is this spring that completely determines intermediate pressure, but because the first stage is open for ambient pressure it compensates for the actual depth—intermediate pressure is therefore a constant pressure above the ambient pressure. On the surface, intermediate pressure for most regulators is 10 bar/145 psi. When you dive the intermediate pressure is 10 bar/145 psi plus the water pressure at the actual depth.

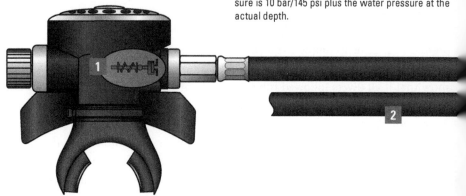

Rinse thoroughly

The outside of the regulator is easy to wash. Be extra careful with the inside of the second stage and the openings on most first stages that are designed to compensate for water pressure (see page 110 onwards). Deposits are easily accumulated in this area and can interfere with the function of the regulator.

O-rings

O-rings do not normally wear, but if your first stage starts to bubble from any of these areas either one of the hoses is loose or the O-ring is damaged and must be replaced.

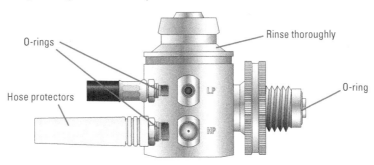

O-rings

Rinse thoroughly

O-ring

Hose protectors

LP

HP

5. Intermediate pressure gauge

This works as a stethoscope for the regulator—you can get a good picture of how it is doing by checking the intermediate pressure and how it varies when you breathe. Intermediate pressure should decrease rapidly when you inhale and return to the set value quickly when you stop.

6. To submersible pressure gauge

Most divers still choose a traditional pressure gauge with a hose to the regulator first stage. Another option is a wireless model where a transmitter on the first stage sends information to the dive computer on your wrist or inside your mask. To facilitate storage of the regulator and to avoid damage to the pressure gauge—especially if you have a console with a dive computer—there are quick-release couplings on the market for the high-pressure hose.

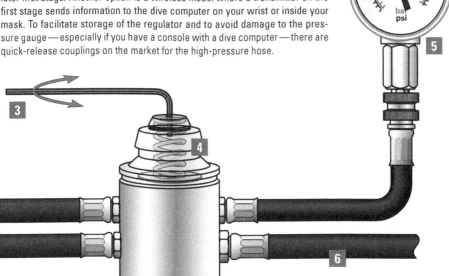

CHAPTER 6

Instruments

The time, depth and amount of air left in the dive cylinder are all bits of information divers need for their own safety. This data can be obtained in different ways and the electronic revolution has had an impact on our way of planning and implementing dives.

In order to plan and implement safe dives we have an interest in getting some information about our equipment and surroundings. Some of this information is necessary, even vital, while some is only given to facilitate decisions or because it may be of interest to us. In diving , we have also been affected by the information focus that prevails in the rest of society, which manifests itself in increasingly sophisticated electronic instruments with more and more features. The only things we really *need* to know are dive time, depth and tank pressure.

Instruments	Time	Depth	Tank Pressure	Heading	Dive Planning
Analogue watch					
Digital watch		Usually			
Analogue pressure gauge					
Analogue depth gauge					
Analogue compass					
Bottom timer	Usually some form of log book function				
Dive computer					Algorithm that calculates dive parameters and enables dive planning
— with tank pressure sensor					
— with electronic compass					

Traditional analogue instruments only have one function, while electronic instruments have two or more. Many modern dive computers replace all the instruments, having an electronic compass, depth gauge and a connection to the first stage — wireless or hose — to also measure tank pressure.

Depth Gauge

To plan our dive we must know the depth we intend to dive to since this is one of the parameters of the dive tables. So, it is important to carry an accurate and reliable depth gauge. Some divers prefer to have their depth gauge on the wrist, but most carry it in a console together with the pressure gauge and compass.

The only way to measure true depth is to have a tape measure from the surface. This is, of course, not particularly convenient, so we choose instead to measure the pressure and then view this as a depth. With this strategy, there are some sources of error, in particular differences in air pressure on the surface, and because salt water and fresh water do not have equal density. These sources of error are, however, only within a few percent, so they are considered to be negligible, especially in view of the safety margins added in planning and implementation.

There are some different design principles for depth gauges, but all of them are essentially a pressure gauge that shows zero depth on the surface (when the pressure is 1 ATM ≈ 1 bar).

Capillary depth gauges

This is the simplest form of depth gauge, with no moving parts. It consists only of a bent plastic tube that is fitted to a disc with depth markings. During descent, air in the tube is compressed according to Boyle's Law and we read how far the water has reached into the tube.

This gives you a very accurate depth gauge at shallow depths, but the markings get closer to each other the deeper you go. So its accuracy decreases with increasing depth. The plastic tube can also become clogged by sand and salt. The advantages are of course the simple design and that it automatically compensates for decreased atmospheric pressure at higher altitudes.

It is rather difficult to find capillary depth gauges since few manufacturers still make them. This diver is at approximately 17 m/56 ft.

Bourdon tube

This is the most common general design for modern depth gauges. An open Bourdon tube is a copper or brass tube that is sealed at one end. An increase in ambient pressure makes the tube straighten and this movement is transferred via gears to the needle.

The disadvantage with this design is that water enters the tube, so deposits can affect the function. To avoid this, some models have a plastic lining on the inside of the tube. This design is no longer common.

To increase reliability and to make the depth gauge more maintenance free, some advanced designs try to keep water from entering the Bourdon tube. A closed Bourdon tube is filled with a liquid and sealed with a flexible diaphragm. This makes it pressure sensing just like an open Bourdon tube, but without the problem of deposits on the inside.

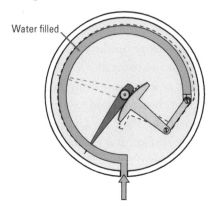

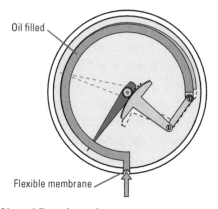

Open Bourdon tube
Water will enter the tube, which means that dirt and deposits are collected over time. This type is now unusual for diving.

Closed Bourdon tube
To reduce the problems with the open Bourdon tube, the tube on this model is closed with a flexible membrane that transmits pressure differences.

Diaphragm depth gauge

This design is based on a flexible bottom that curves with increased ambient pressure. Pressure changes are transferred with the help of an arm that sits against the flexible bottom. This design is also fully closed, so it requires no real maintenance other than that it must be rinsed on the outside after each dive.

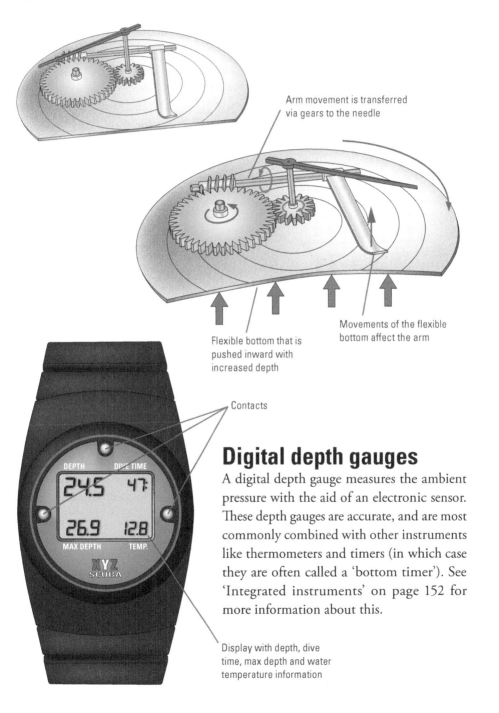

Arm movement is transferred via gears to the needle

Movements of the flexible bottom affect the arm

Flexible bottom that is pushed inward with increased depth

Contacts

Display with depth, dive time, max depth and water temperature information

Digital depth gauges

A digital depth gauge measures the ambient pressure with the aid of an electronic sensor. These depth gauges are accurate, and are most commonly combined with other instruments like thermometers and timers (in which case they are often called a 'bottom timer'). See 'Integrated instruments' on page 152 for more information about this.

Characteristics

There are some general features to consider when you choose a depth gauge. These are common for all models except capillary depth gauges and include:

- **Maximum-depth indicator** — This needle follows the main needle during the descent, but it stays at the deepest depth reached during the dive. During the ascent the depth gauge shows both the actual depth and the deepest depth. A common complaint is that they show greater depths than you believe you dived to … they are not a replacement for paying close attention to your depth!
- **Altitude adjustment** — A depth gauge is a pressure gauge showing zero at 1 atm (sea level). So we must be able to adjust it if we want to dive at high altitude, where the surface pressure will be lower than at sea level. Normally this is done with a small thumb wheel that rotates the dial.
- **Fluorescent dial** — This is especially important for night diving, but a fluorescent dial can also be helpful during the day in poor visibility.

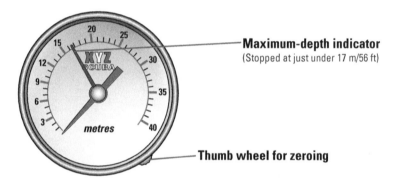

Maximum-depth indicator
(Stopped at just under 17 m/56 ft)

Thumb wheel for zeroing

Accuracy

Electronic depth gauges are often accurate to within 15 cm/6 in and this does not change over time. A mechanical depth gauge is less accurate and exhaustion of the material means its accuracy decreases with time and dives. For this reason it is important to check depth gauges regularly, for example before a new season, to be sure they show the correct depth (see page 154). If they do not, they are difficult to calibrate. Instead, you must be aware of the problem and the amount of deviation. If the discrepancy is large, you should buy a new depth gauge.

EN 13319: Diving accessories — Depth Gauges and combined depth and time measuring devices — Functional and safety requirements, test methods

This EU directive states that an increase in pressure of 1 bar must give an increase of shown depth of 10 metres. The rule is based on a density of 1.0197 kg/l. This means that the actual water depth in fresh water (1.00 kg/l) is 102% of displayed value and in sea water (1.03 kg/l) 99% of shown value. Many electronic depth gauges and dive computers can be set to actual type of water, otherwise the above applies.

Pressure Gauge

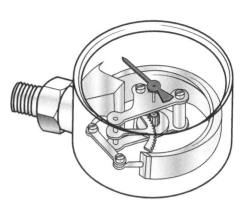

Time and depth are essential information for most types of diving, in order to prevent decompression sickness. The pressure in your tank is unrelated to decompression sickness, unless you run out of air and have to make an emergency ascent. While it is possible to get a warning of low air with a *reserve valve* (see page 104), there might not be enough air in the reserve to return to the surface with a safety stop. The advantage with a submersible pressure gauge (SPG) is that we know exactly how much air we have in the tank at any stage of the dive and we can use this information to aid our decision making.

A pressure gauge normally consists of an ordinary Bourdon tube that is connected to the first stage with a high-pressure hose. The hose has a reduction in the end that connects to the first stage to reduce the flow of air in the unlikely event of a hose rupture. So if the high pressure hose breaks the flow of air will be limited.

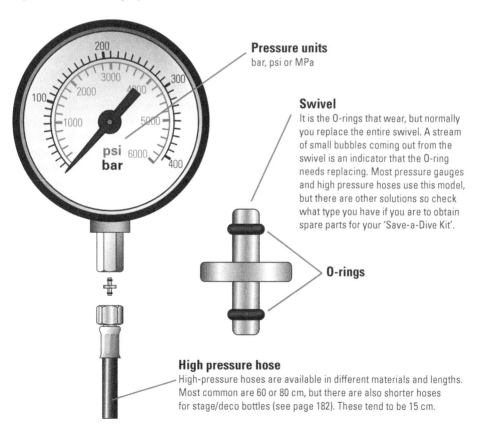

Pressure units
bar, psi or MPa

Swivel
It is the O-rings that wear, but normally you replace the entire swivel. A stream of small bubbles coming out from the swivel is an indicator that the O-ring needs replacing. Most pressure gauges and high pressure hoses use this model, but there are other solutions so check what type you have if you are to obtain spare parts for your 'Save-a-Dive Kit'.

O-rings

High pressure hose
High-pressure hoses are available in different materials and lengths. Most common are 60 or 80 cm, but there are also shorter hoses for stage/deco bottles (see page 182). These tend to be 15 cm.

A common problem is an air leak from the swivel in the connection between the hose and the pressure gauge (see page 147). To avoid problems with the internal mechanism most pressure gauges are fitted with an over-pressure relief valve on the reverse of the casing. The plug will go instead of the glass breaking. Still, it is recommended that you do not look straight at the glass when opening the cylinder valve.

Just as with mechanical *depth* gauges, the metal in mechanical *pressure* gauges will eventually, gradually be exhausted. This means that accuracy will decrease over time and use, so it is important to compare your pressure gauge with an accurate one once in a while, for example the calibrated pressure gauge on the filling ramp of a compressor.

The most common unit on pressure gauges in Europe is *bar*, but on the American market *psi* (pounds per square inch) dominates. In the past, MPa (Mega Pascal) was used in some locations. This is actually the most accurate unit according to the metric system.

Pascal (Pa)	bar	psi	atm
100,000	1	14.5038	0.986923
6,894.76	0.0689476	1	0.0680460
101,325	1.01325	14.6959	1

MPa/bar/psi conversion

Pressure is defined as the force per unit area, which **can be written as: $p = F/A$**, where p is the pressure, F is force and A surface. The SI unit* for pressure is Newton per square metre (N/m^2), which is called Pascal (Pa).** Because Pascal is a small unit, it is used with prefixes to reduce the number of digits:

Hekto = 100 (10^2)
Kilo = 1,000 (10^3)
Mega = 1,000,000 (10^6)

20 Mega Pascal (MPa) is 20,000,000 or 20 million Pa.

In the pressure conversion table you will see that 1 bar is equal to 100,000 Pa. A cylinder filled to 200 bar would show 20 MPa.

Example 1
How many psi is 200 bar? 200 × 14.5038 = **2901 psi**

Example 2
How many bar is 3000 psi? 3000 × 0.0689476 = **206.84 bar** or 3000/14.5038 = **206.84 bar**

For rough calculations, it is easier to use a ratio of **1 bar = 15 psi**

* SI are the units included in the international system of units (SI — *Le Système International d'Unités*), a standard for units where the seven basic units of measurement are accurately defined. It is also known as the metric system.
** Blaise Pascal lived in France in the mid 1600s. He died at the age of 39. He was a mathematician, physicist, philosopher and author of religious publications.

There are now also electronic pressure gauges. These are normally integrated with a dive computer, either through a high pressure hose or via a small transmitter on the first stage. See 'Integrated instruments' on page 152 for more information about this.

Time Keeping

Time is a crucial factor for dive planning. Without the means to check the time, you can't follow dive tables and would therefore have no ability to check if you were diving within safe limits to avoid decompressions sickness. Without something to keep the time you must stay shallow (no deeper than 5 m/16 ft) or with a person that has one. Both options are undesirable and not recommended by any training agency.

A good dive watch should naturally fulfil all the demands put on a normal watch, plus some extra things for divers: e.g. a flexible strap that fits over the suit, large numbers, light or luminescent display and scratch resistant glass.

In addition to displaying the correct time, the most important feature for a diving watch is that it must be waterproof. This is defined in different ways, but a diving watch should be classed for 200 metres. Very few dive to anything like that depth, but that is not the key significance of the depth rating: watches with this depth rating are designed to cope with the additional pressure placed on them when entering the water and when moving around at depth.

Analogue dive watches also have a bezel that can only be turned in one direction. This is used to show when the dive started and how long you have been down. It can only be turned in one direction so as to avoid unintentionally staying longer than you plan.

Analogue dive watch

Fluorescent markings

Bezel

Rated for 200 m

Dive watch with digital depth gauge

Current depth

Depth sensor

This diver has been down 35 minutes

Strap

Many divers replace the strap with a Velcro band. This is a more flexible solution as many bracelets won't fit over a diving suit. Another advantage of having a strap that goes under both pins is the reduced risk of dropping the watch—if you lose one pin the strap remains under the other one.

Digital watches have a stopwatch function instead, so you see exactly how long you have dived. Digital watches are often equipped with other functions like a depth gauge, memory for the greatest depth, etc. There are also digital depth gauges with analogue display of the time.

Compass

In many areas of the world a compass is an essential instrument for underwater navigation, but for many divers it is an accessory that is rarely used. Most models are completely mechanical, with a needle in a liquid-filled casing.

Accuracy is good and they are simple to use, especially those compasses that have a small side window for a better view of the bearing while swimming. Viewed from above it is shown on the bezel, provided you line it up so that north falls in the index notch. First, turn yourself until the red or black lubber line points to the desired bearing. Make a mental note of the bearing.

Bezel

Index marks

Magnetic north needle

Lubber line

Sighting notch

Side window

In our digital era, we naturally have electronic compasses too. These are accurate and can, as with all other electronic instruments, be combined with other functions. More and more dive computers have them built-in. Some divers prefer to have a compass on their wrist, but it is common to have it together with pressure and depth gauges in a console. Having the compass on the wrist makes it easier to navigate with high accuracy by keeping it away from metal items of dive kit.

Dive Computer

Computers not only combine time-keeping and depth gauge, but are also advanced interpreters of dive tables. They measure actual depth and dive time. They then calculate your available bottom time and any decompression needed. As you change depths the dive computer recalculates and updates the information. After the dive it logs the surface interval and predicts the no decompression limit (NDL) for the next dive. The computer can also give the time before it is considered safe to fly.

Puck-style dive computer

These have clear and easy-to-read displays with relevant information before, during and after the dive. Some models are adaptable and can be used on the wrist or in a console.

Watch-style dive computer

This is a handy solution. Some models include an electronic compass and can be set for breathing gases other than air. But most importantly; you get a stylish watch that you can wear in everyday life — the dive computer is always with you!

A dive computer makes it easier to conduct a dive, but unfortunately many divers use these fantastic instruments carelessly. It is important to realize that a dive computer is not a replacement for prudent dive planning — it only tells us how long we can stay at the actual depth. It is also important to understand that the dive computer uses algorithms based on dive tables and other scientific models. There are a number of different algorithms — at least seven — being used in current models of dive computers at the time of writing. Each of these produces slightly different results depending on how conservative the algorithm is. The main problem with pushing a dive computer's profile to the limit is that computers only calculate time at depth. They do not take into consideration other risk factors such as how fit you are or the rate you use your air, although models which claim to do some of this are starting to appear on the market. These factors also influence your risk of decompression sickness (DCS). It is important to realize that even by following a computer you can still get the bends. You should always dive a little more conservatively than your computer requires. Some models of dive computer allow you to adjust how conservative the algorithm setting is, to increase the safety margin.

It is important to read the manual carefully before you use a dive computer and to learn what it really displays. A good way to do this is to use one of the excellent simulation programmes that most manufacturers have for their computers. With the aid of an ordinary personal computer, you can simulate different dive profiles to see how the nitrogen absorbs into the tissues, is distributed in the body and released during ascent and during the surface interval. With the right interface you can also transfer information between your dive computer and personal computer so you can see what happened during real dives. This feature can also be used to keep an electronic log book, although it is still wise to keep a paper copy in case of data corruption.

Most dive computers can be set for diving on nitrox mixes ranging from 21% (air) to 50%. There are models for trimix diving—where helium is in the gas mixture for deep diving (usually deeper than 40 m/130 ft). Some models allow for 'gas switching'—changing gas mixture under water so that the computer can continue to monitor your decompression penalty when you change gas from air or trimix to nitrox. This is useful for technical/decompression diving and not something that most beginners need concern themselves with.

Integrated instruments

All these analogue functions (timer, depth gauge, pressure gauge, compass) can also be found in electronic instruments and normally combined in some form. The simplest electronic instrument is a bottom timer. This primarily shows time and depth, but may also display information like temperature, maximum depth, etc. It can also have a limited log book function that saves information about the last few dives. These instruments are often very reliable and good value, so they are a good alternative to a separate dive watch and depth gauge.

There are also dive computers with integrated pressure gauges. The advantage is that you not only get information about your cylinder pressure, the computer also calculates how long the air will last at the actual depth with your present breathing rate. They either come with a high-pressure hose to the first stage, or they are wireless. Hose models look like ordinary instrument consoles but with only one digital display with all the information gathered together. The alternative is a wireless transmitter connected to the first stage that transfers the information to a computer on the diver's wrist. Remember that you then have two batteries to take into account—one in the dive computer and one in the sensor.

Air integrated dive computer with hose
This solution is becoming less and less common, but it is a much more robust solution than wireless transmission of a signal from the first stage. A hose is not dependent on the signal and you only have to maintain one battery.

Computer with large colourful display, compass and cylinder integration

Fully integrated computers are available in both small wrist models, puck-style and even larger ones with clear colourful graphics. All integrated wrist models get cylinder pressure via a wireless sensor installed on the regulator first stage.

Wireless sensor/transmitter attachment

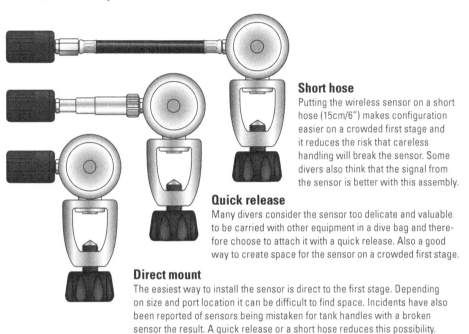

Short hose

Putting the wireless sensor on a short hose (15cm/6") makes configuration easier on a crowded first stage and it reduces the risk that careless handling will break the sensor. Some divers also think that the signal from the sensor is better with this assembly.

Quick release

Many divers consider the sensor too delicate and valuable to be carried with other equipment in a dive bag and therefore choose to attach it with a quick release. Also a good way to create space for the sensor on a crowded first stage.

Direct mount

The easiest way to install the sensor is direct to the first stage. Depending on size and port location it can be difficult to find space. Incidents have also been reported of sensors being mistaken for tank handles with a broken sensor the result. A quick release or a short hose reduces this possibility.

Heads-up display (HUD) mask

The latest addition to the development of both diving mask and dive computer.

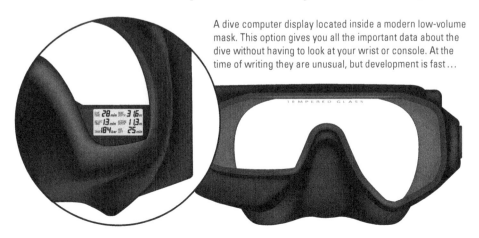

A dive computer display located inside a modern low-volume mask. This option gives you all the important data about the dive without having to look at your wrist or console. At the time of writing they are unusual, but development is fast ...

Smartphone

There are a few solutions that enable you to use your smartphone as a dive computer. This is based, of course, on a waterproof shell, so it will be significantly larger than a typical dive computer. But then you really get a fully integrated tool with all the smartphone benefits in addition to the usual dive computer — handy

electronic log book, camera, camcorder and ability to share your experiences on the internet/social media without connecting to a personal computer.

Computer interface

Most dive computers can be connected to a personal computer via a specific interface. This allows you to have an electronic logbook, analyse your dives and change dive computer settings in an easier manner. It is highly illustrative to look at how the nitrogen levels of the different compartments (fast and slow tissues) vary during a dive.

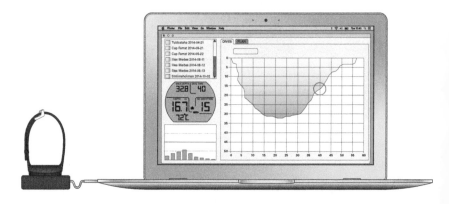

Care and Maintenance

Modern electronic instruments are so sophisticated that only trained professionals can service them. Some models allow you to change the battery, although dive shops may also be able to pressure-test the device. Mechanical depth and pressure gauges, compasses, and watches seldom fail, but their accuracy must be regularly checked. A depth gauge can be checked against a dive computer or bottom timer and the accuracy of a pressure gauge against the precise gauge on a filling ramp. The most common problem with pressure gauges is leaks from where they swivel, between the gauge and the hose (see page 147). Rinse all instruments after diving.

CHAPTER 7

Weight Systems

Naked in the water most people are close to neutrally buoyant, but with dive gear on this changes. It is mainly our suits that make us positively buoyant, and as we usually have one on we need to compensate to be able to dive. So, we almost always need some form of additional weighting.

Lead is an ideal metal for diving weights since it has very high density, is easy to shape and does not corrode. For a long time weight belts came in one simple design: a 50 mm/2 in wide nylon band, a buckle and some cast lead weights from 1–6 kg/ 2–13 lbs in size. Over the years, more features have been developed so it is worth looking at these when deciding which system to choose.

Weight Belts

Buckle—This must be designed to be opened with one hand, normally the right hand. There are some different designs on the market, but the standard buckle is the most common. All of these have the same function and it should be possible to ditch the belt with one hand in an emergency. So it is important not to tuck the free end under the belt if you have a standard buckle.

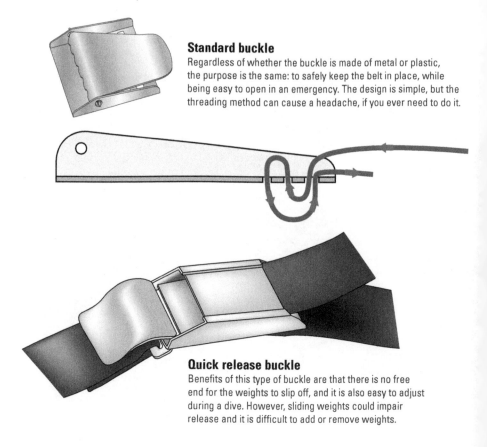

Standard buckle
Regardless of whether the buckle is made of metal or plastic, the purpose is the same: to safely keep the belt in place, while being easy to open in an emergency. The design is simple, but the threading method can cause a headache, if you ever need to do it.

Quick release buckle
Benefits of this type of buckle are that there is no free end for the weights to slip off, and it is also easy to adjust during a dive. However, sliding weights could impair release and it is difficult to add or remove weights.

Belt—The nylon belt should be 50 mm/2 in wide and the length should be adjusted for body size and the amount of weights so that the free end is not too long or too short.

Weights—Normally cast in an alloy of lead and some other metals these come in many shapes and sizes. You also find plastic-coated weights. This makes them look more attractive and reduces wear on boat decks, etc. In some areas, you can find weights in imaginative shapes and colours like pink hearts or black hand grenades.

Weight retainers—To stop weights from sliding around on the belt. These are threaded onto the belt and hold the weights in place.

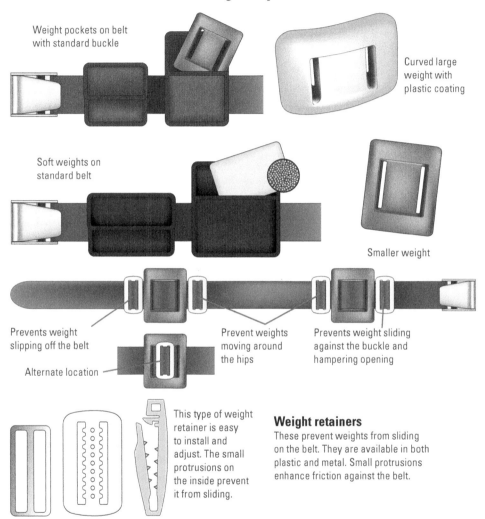

Weight pockets on belt with standard buckle

Curved large weight with plastic coating

Soft weights on standard belt

Smaller weight

Prevents weight slipping off the belt

Alternate location

Prevent weights moving around the hips

Prevents weight sliding against the buckle and hampering opening

This type of weight retainer is easy to install and adjust. The small protrusions on the inside prevent it from sliding.

Weight retainers

These prevent weights from sliding on the belt. They are available in both plastic and metal. Small protrusions enhance friction against the belt.

Shot belts are popular. Instead of big hard weights, this system uses one or more pockets in ballistic nylon filled with lead shot. The pockets shape themselves around your body, so a shot belt is much more comfortable to dive with, especially if you need a lot of lead to be neutrally buoyant underwater. The disadvantage is that you need to be more careful with them since a small hole can result in losing your lead shot all over the boat deck. No fun!

Integrated Weights

Since the introduction of modern back-mounted BCDs, more and more solutions for integrated weight systems have been developed. This means that you don't need to have any weights on a belt around your waist, but instead they can be connected to the BCD in some way. You must still be able to ditch them in an emergency, so they always have some kind of quick-release mechanism.

Normally, you put the weights in two separate pockets, one on each side, so you can choose to ditch only one or both to get some positive buoyancy. The advantages include having everything gathered in one compact set and most divers also find it easier on their back, especially if they need a lot of lead. However, you may find it uncomfortable to have all the lead in the BCD, especially when exiting from the water, or that there is not enough room for all your lead (there is usually a capacity of around 3–4 kg/6–9 lbs per pocket). Then you need both a traditional weight belt *and* integrated weights.

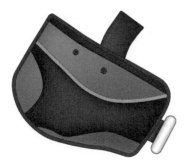 

Pockets take a quick-release insert which holds the weights, which do not need holes for a belt.

Special Weights

Ankle weights—These are sometimes used by drysuit divers to avoid having too much air at their feet. However, this is mainly a compensation for poor technique. It is better to learn how to dive in a drysuit, for example by attending a drysuit course. With 0.5–1.0 kg/1–2 lbs of lead around your ankles to lift with each fin kick, during the course of a dive you lift quite a lot, with higher air consumption the result. Another option is to use heavy fins (see page 32) or to work on your diving skills so you don't need any extra weight around your ankles.

Ankle weight

An argument in favour of ankle weights is that they can be used to distribute weight more evenly, but it is still more weight lifted with each and every fin stroke and there are better ways of distributing weight, such as:

Wedged or **'V-weights'** — are placed between the cylinders to adjust the balance of twin tanks. Take extra care with your back if you choose to make the whole assembly even heavier with these.

Weight with hook — can be used to temporarily adjust balance, for example, when you try new equipment or dive in a new environment. They can also be used upside-down — with this weight on the belt you have a hook to attach accessories to.

Small weight with hook

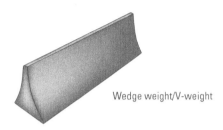

Wedge weight/V-weight

Harness

In colder waters (with bulkier thermal protection) you need more lead to be neutrally buoyant, so this may be a more comfortable solution. The weights are carried on a separate harness in pockets which have a quick release function.

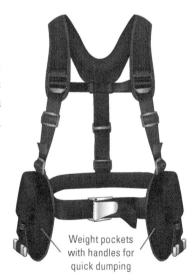

Weight pockets with handles for quick dumping

Care and Maintenance

Weights are probably the items of kit which need the least care — rather the rest of your kit needs protection from them! Integrated weight pockets can get damaged and eventually wear out, so inspect them occasionally. The same applies to shot weight bags. Plastic coatings can be damaged by mistreatment and eventually crack and break. However, the lead will still do its job without them.

CHAPTER 8

Accessories

The equipment discussed so far can largely be considered essential. But there is also a lot of other equipment that facilitates diving, increases safety or makes it easier to accomplish specific tasks. This list is far from complete but in this chapter we look at the most common activities.

Lights

When it is dark outside, we use a torch to be able to see well. A dive torch has the same use when we dive at night, but it is also useful during the day. The deeper you go, the more natural colours are lost, but if you take the sun down with you, you can bring out the true colours again. In addition, you can use a dive torch to light up small cracks and holes to see what is hiding inside them.

A good torch for diving must be waterproof, powerful (preferably), and the batteries must last for a bare minimum of an hour — i.e. one 'normal' dive. In reality most last a lot longer. There are a lot of different models to choose between, everything from big powerful torches with separate battery-packs to small lights that can be carried in a BCD pocket.

Main dive torch

The main torch is your primary light source during night diving and other diving where light is limited, for example inside wrecks and caves. These lights are too large to put in a BCD so they often have a handle and some way to fasten them to a BCD.

Most main diving torches have rechargeable battery packs and come with a charger. On some models, it is possible to set the angle of light but usually the manufacturer has specified the light pattern and thus balance between bright light in the centre (spot) and broad lighting (flood). Some models also provide choice with replaceable lamp 'heads' with alternative beam angle, light strength, and source.

A typical main light with LED technology has a luminous flux of 1,000 lumens and upwards. Many main dive torches have variable light output, so you can adjust the light according to the conditions and save on batteries. When diving in poor visibility, a large luminous flux will give the same effect as driving a car with headlights in fog — it will be milky white.

Back-up torch/day torch

This is a fairly simple dive torch. A suitable back-up/day torch should be quite small but still provide enough light for you to be able to finish a night dive if the main light stops working.

There are many models of LED lamps to choose from, most use interchangeable batteries of the AAA or AA sizes.

If the back-up /day torch is too big to be stored in a BCD pocket, you must find a way to attach it so that you do not need to hold it during the entire dive. It should have a good wrist strap so that you won't lose it if you drop it.

A typical back-up/day torch with LED technology has a luminous flux of 200 to 500 lumens.

Modular/canister torches

In canister torches, the designers have chosen to separate the light source and battery pack. Development in this direction was driven by the need for brighter light sources for technical diving, and thus the requirement for greater battery capacity. A battery canister is normally attached to your cylinder or wing (BCD) harness. The small lamp head is attached to the wrist with Velcro straps or held with a Goodman handle.

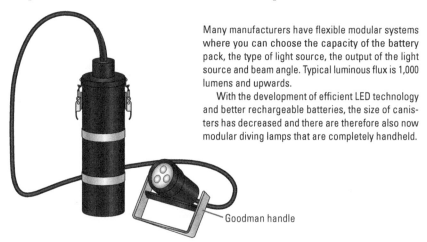

Many manufacturers have flexible modular systems where you can choose the capacity of the battery pack, the type of light source, the output of the light source and beam angle. Typical luminous flux is 1,000 lumens and upwards.

With the development of efficient LED technology and better rechargeable batteries, the size of canisters has decreased and there are therefore also now modular diving lamps that are completely handheld.

Goodman handle

Features

Brightness

If you only use the torch to look in cracks and crevices during the day, it is not necessary to have a strong light, but for night diving, wreck diving or cave diving you must have a bright torch. Traditionally, all bulbs were rated in watts, but this is not a measure of how much light the bulb provides. Instead, it is the effect, which, together with the time gives the energy consumption. This was not a major problem as long as bulbs were based on incandescent technique, but with the greater use of LED lights we have to use other ways to measure light (see page 163).

Type of light source

Development is fast when it comes to light sources and mainly LED (Light Emitting Diode). For the vast majority of divers, this is the best option regardless of the type of dive torch. This statement is also supported by what is available on the market—most manufacturers have stopped producing dive torches with light sources other than LED. The great efficiency of LED technology has made it possible to reduce the size of dive torches and yet increase the light yield, so we see both smaller and more efficient models. Some technical divers prefer to use high intensity discharge (HID) lamps due to their high output power, but these dive torches are becoming increasingly rare.

Light source	Gas-discharge light (HID)	Light emitting diode (LED)
Appearance		
Efficiency	Approximately 50–80 lumens per watt depending on the type.	Very efficient, up to over 100 lumens per watt. When the light is directed, the brightness becomes greater compared with other light sources with the same luminous flux.
Life	10,000 hours during normal use. Frequent switching on and off will reduce lifespan.	More than 20,000 hours, but the efficiency decreases with time.
Colour temperature	Between 4,100 K and 6,000 K depending on which metal salts are inside the bulb.	Available spanning a range of colours, between 3,000 K and 5,500 K.
Temperature	Efficiency is better than halogen bulbs, so they are not as hot.	LED lights get hot, but the heat is not radiated, instead it must be directed away from the metal in the unit.

Measures of light

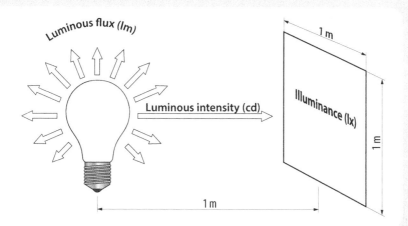

Brightness—or **luminous intensity**—is a measure of how much light shines in a certain direction from a light source. The international unit of brightness is **candelas** and has the abbreviation 'cd'. A common candle emits light with roughly 1 cd luminous intensity and this is how candela was first defined. The unit is now more accurately determined.

Luminous flux is the measure of perceived power of light and the international unit is **lumen** (lm). You can think of luminous flux as the total amount of visible light present. This is the standard now used to compare the useful light emitted by different light sources.

Illuminance is a measure of the intensity of illumination on a surface, which is measured in lux (lumens per square metre). The illuminance depends on the orientation and the distance between the illuminated surface and the light source.

Colour temperature

Colour temperature is measured in degrees Kelvin — the higher the number the whiter (colder) the light. LED lights normally provide a whiter light compared to old-fashioned incandescent lamps. This can be both an advantage and disadvantage when diving. A warmer light also provides warmer colours for the highlights, while a colder light reaches further underwater because it has more energy.

Incandescent	Warm White	Cool White	Daylight
2700 K	3000 K	4000 K	6000 K

Batteries

The higher the power of the light source the more battery capacity you need. If it doesn't come with the equipment it is normally worth the investment to get rechargeable batteries for your main light. It is also important to investigate if it is possible to recharge batteries at your normal dive destination(s). On charter boats and at many remote tropical destinations, two or three small holes in the wall are not something you can take for granted. Solar-powered chargers might be worth considering for some situations.

Switch

It would be difficult to use a light without a switch, so this is an obvious part, but also the biggest trouble for torch designers. The more moving parts in a design for underwater use, the bigger the risk of leaks. On smaller lights the front cap is normally rotated to switch on and off. The key to this is one or two O-rings which give a good and secure seal.

Variations

As already mentioned, modular systems allow you to change the torch head to get a different kind of light. There are also some torches on the market which have different settings — you can vary the brightness for instance. This can be useful for conserving battery power and avoiding upsetting sensitive wildlife. A flashing/SOS mode is a handy safety feature should you ever be lost on the surface.

How many dive torches should I have?

During night diving you should normally carry two or more lights: one main light and back-ups. So consider buying more than one model. The back-up light doesn't need to be as powerful as the main light and will also be usable for day diving.

In some areas glowsticks are used during night diving to identify divers. These are safe and run without batteries. The disadvantage is that they are not particularly environmentally friendly and the cost can be high if you dive at night a lot.

It is better to buy a battery-powered light stick that fulfils the same function at a much more environmentally-friendly price. These are available in different colours, so it is possible to clearly mark individual divers and the ascent line.

Knives/Line Cutters

If you look at the size of many diving knives you might be led to believe that they are primarily weapons. This is not the case, the diving knife is a tool used for picking, digging, and measuring. You face a minimal risk of entanglement underwater, so it is also useful for cutting yourself loose from fishing nets or line, and seaweed or kelp. For this reason it is important to ensure the knife remains sharp and that it has a serrated edge, since this is actually more useful underwater.

Dive knives should be made of stainless steel but this is a problem since the choice of steel alloy is a compromise between the degree of stainlessness and sharpness. It is important that you take care of your knife so it will not corrode. Regular cleaning, oiling and sharpening are key, but check what the manufacturer recommends. Some knives are made of titanium, which is as hard as steel, but does not corrode and is significantly lighter (and more expensive).

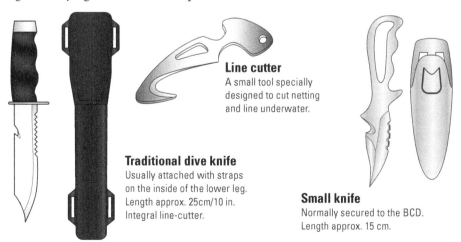

Line cutter
A small tool specially designed to cut netting and line underwater.

Traditional dive knife
Usually attached with straps on the inside of the lower leg. Length approx. 25cm/10 in. Integral line-cutter.

Small knife
Normally secured to the BCD. Length approx. 15 cm.

There are many ways to fasten a dive knife to your kit, but—just as for the weight belt—it is important that you can reach it with one hand. The classic position is strapped inside the lower leg, reducing the risk of entanglement. However, as this is further away from the hands many consider that inside the triangle attached to the BCD is a better place (see page 131). Large knives are becoming rare for general diving—small knives incorporating line cutters are just as useful and easier to attach to the BCD.

Knives are not allowed in all locations—some marine reserves specifically ban them. Listen to your dive guide or seek other local advice if diving in unfamiliar areas.

Flags

We share our interest in water activities with many others including fishermen, sailors and water-skiers. Since we are not clearly visible from the surface, we have to show water users were we are and what we are doing.

International maritime rules state that when we are diving from an *anchored* vessel or one with restricted movement because it has to stay near its divers, the International Code of Signals 'Alpha' flag must be flown. It must be shown as a screen (fully shown) even in light winds, with the shortest side at least 1 m/3 ft. Passing ships shall, if possible, disengage their propeller. The screen must be visible around the horizon and be illuminated during the hours of darkness. If the vessel is longer than 12 metres, the following lights must also be used: three all-around lights mounted vertically—the top and bottom light red and the one in the middle white.[1]

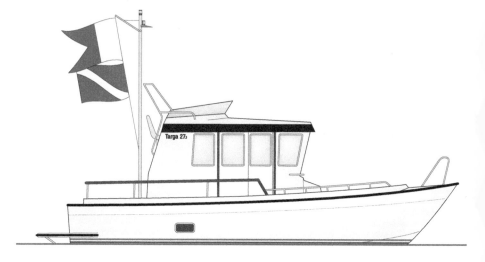

---

1   *International Regulations for Preventing Collisions at Sea 1972 (Colregs)* published by the International Maritime Organization (IMO). Rule 27, paragraphs d, e and g.

The *Colregs* say nothing about scuba diving specifically, but many national regulations indicate that these rules also apply when scuba diving. Diving from land is not mentioned, these rules are to avoid collisions at sea.

It is a great mistake to believe that all boats keep a wide berth when the Alpha flag is shown. There is no statement in the rules about how close a boat may pass or how close to their vessel divers should stay. It is also far from all water users who know what the Alpha flag means. The recommendation is to be protective and select dive spots with care, especially during the summer.

In the United States and in areas influenced by the US, the Alpha flag is less common and many divers in these areas don't even know what it means. Instead, a red-white flag called 'Divers Down' is used to alert others of diving. The meaning is largely the same, but as the Divers Down flag is not in the *Colregs* any legislation is local or non-existent.

It is therefore, as ever, important to find out what applies locally where you dive. The Alpha flag is always right, but in many areas the red flag is also mentioned in local regulations, for example, the individual US states all have their own interpretations. These can include how close divers must keep to the flag and how large a distance other boats must keep from the flag.

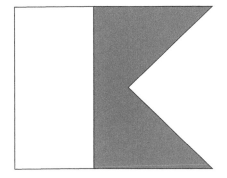

Alpha flag
As defined by the International Code of Signals (ICS), the code flag A means 'I have a diver down; keep well clear at slow speed'.

Diver Down
This flag has been developed to protect divers in the water (as opposed to the Alpha flag the purpose of which is to stop vessels colliding). It is not mentioned in any international regulations or conventions, so it is up to local authorities, who often include rules on distance for divers and boats.

More information about flags is available at Dive Flag Law: www.dive-flag.com/law.html

Signal/Surface Marker Buoys

These are used to alert other water users to where (underwater) divers are. The buoys can either be used stationary, anchored to the bottom or taken with divers wherever they go. The elongated version better suits being dragged by moving or drifting divers. Whichever type is used, it is connected via a thin line (usually on a reel, see page 169) held by one diver in a pair or group and is suitable for use when the divers cover a large area or if entry and exit is in different places.

Surface marker buoys
On the left a buoy that is more suitable for stationary activities. To the right a streamlined model that is suitable to be dragged on the surface. Both are available with either an Alpha flag or Diver Down.

Delayed surface marker buoy
Usually much taller and therefore more visible than an SMB. See below regarding colours.

Safety sausage/delayed surface marker buoy (DSMB)/deco buoy

A delayed surface marker buoy is an approximately 2 m/6.5 ft long 'sausage' in a clearly visible colour, usually yellow-green or orange-red. It is stored rolled and attached to the BCD or in a leg pocket during a dive. When you need to use it, you inflate it with either your mouth, extra second stage, inflation hose, or a small dedicated cylinder (depending on the model, your training and your preference). Usually a small weight at the lower end keeps it upright in the water, or it is attached to a reel.

There are a variety of uses for surface markers and use varies by location and boat captain, usually dependent on the current and the amount of local boat traffic:

1. To show your presence to the boat captain during or when you surface after a drift dive. Many dive centres require this of all divers today, especially when diving at offshore sites or places with strong currents.
2. To mark your position during drift decompression.

The diver must use a thin line attached to the surface marker of sufficient length (50% longer than the deepest depth it will be deployed from, i.e. for 20 m, 30 m of line is needed). This is usually kept in a reel—see next item. For tropical diving some people use 5 m/15 ft of line with a small weight on the end—it can be wrapped around the DSMB when not in use and deployed on the safety stop. Different colours can be used to show the surface organization if everything proceeds according to plan or if a problem has occurred. For example, many divers consider a yellow DSMB to mean there is a problem below, although this is not universally accepted.

Reels

Some diving activities require a thin line, for example search and recovery, wreck penetration and where returning to a specific place (e.g. a shotline) is imperative. It is also necessary for using a surface marker buoy if you intend to release it from all but the shallowest of depths.

The simplest variant is a finger reel. With a bit of practice, this covers most needs. It is important to use the right technique to avoid jams. Keep it attached with a double-ended hook. Hold it between thumb and index finger when deploying it.

A line reel can harbour a longer line than a finger reel and it is easier to use because you wind the line back in with a handle. Line reels also have either a friction brake or a ratchet mechanism to stop the line rolling back out. The disadvantage is the size—they are too big to be stored in a pocket when not in use during the dive.

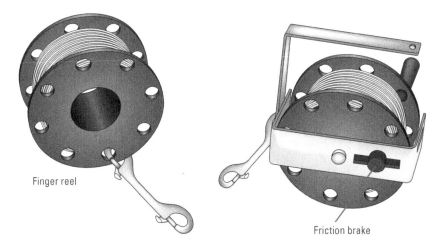

Finger reel

Friction brake

Line markers

When diving in confined spaces like inside wrecks or caves, it may be important to mark specific points especially if the visibility might deteriorate, or in case of torch malfunction. The direction to the exit point can be marked using plastic arrows that are made to be put on your line and you can even use your hands to feel the direction that they point in

Similarly, cookies are round, plastic discs to attach to the line which are used to indicate a junction or change of direction. There are also non-directional markers to reference a specific spot (where something may have been left to collect on the way out for example).

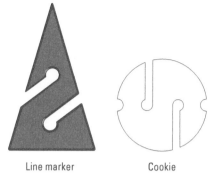

Line marker   Cookie

Buddy Line

This is an excellent way to prevent divers in a buddy team from losing contact with each other. A buddy line is anything from 1.25–3 m/4–10 ft long, made of a synthetic material and some have a small float at the centre to prevent the line from getting stuck in something on the bottom. It is best to have the rope in a sliding knot around the wrist. You can then simply use the rope to draw attention to you buddy if you see something interesting, when it is time to ascend or turn back. It is important that dive planning includes a discussion on how the buddy line will be used, which side you will swim in relation to each other and who leads the dive.

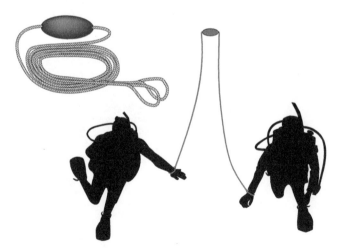

For divers who are accustomed to clear water this might seem both clumsy and strange, you probably have not even have heard of this device, but anyone who has dived in limited visibility appreciates a buddy line and considers it a natural part of their scuba kit. There are some disadvantages: divers could become entangled, and an uncontrolled ascent by one diver could injure the other.

Lifting Bag

Lifting bags are available in various sizes to suit different sizes and weights of objects which might need to be lifted from the seabed. They are made from heavy synthetic materials with straps or loops for attaching ropes. At the top, there is a often a valve to release the expanding air during ascent. Salvaging items is a specialized form of diving that requires proper education, equipment and planning. It is important to also ensure that you adhere to local laws regarding salvage, which is beyond the scope of this book.

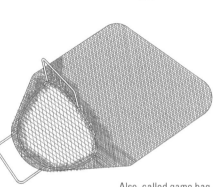

Mesh Bag

A mesh bag can be used for anything from cooling drinks in the water to carrying equipment that cannot be fixed to a BCD in other ways. In areas where it is permitted and appropriate, it may also be used to collect seafood for dinner. Made of open nylon mesh and some are fitted with a rigid opening for easier use underwater.

Also, called game bag, goody bag or catch bag.

Attachment

There are often small items we wish to have with us on a dive but do not want to carry or place in the small pockets (if we have any) of our BCD. These can instead be connected to D-rings on a BCD. For things that do not need to be loosened during the dive it is often sufficient to use a simple snap hook. Be aware that these can be opened accidentally and can catch a rope if you swim against one. Better to use a locking version.

If you need to, for example, remove a reel from a D-ring on your BCD during a dive, it is better to fix this with a trigger hook. These are available in several sizes and models, including double-ended ones. Whatever you choose, it should be made of a material that will not corrode — stainless steel or plastic for lightweight items.

Trigger hook/bolt snap — best

Carabiner — not as good

Coil lanyard

This is a good utility for fixing things that you want to use during the dive, but not lose if you have to drop them, for example a camera.

It consists of two hooks (or any other type of fastening) connected by both a quick release buckle and a plastic coil. The attached accessory is located close to your body. If you want to use it, you just open the quick release buckle and you then have a range of at least an arm's length.

Coil lanyard

Retractor

A retractor is a good way to, for example, attach your instruments to your BCD. They are held close to your body, but when you want to look at them it is easy to move them close to you or to show your buddy/dive guide. Also useful for compasses and small torches. However, they can leave things dangling from your kit, and reduce streamlining.

Retractor

Communication

Our hero Jacques-Yves Cousteau coined the term *The Silent World* with his film and book, but we know that even though there is actually a lot of noise in the water, we cannot normally just talk to each other underwater. It is of course now possible to buy special masks with underwater radios but they are expensive—see 'Full-face mask' on page 26.

Many divers find the quiet relaxing, but sometimes it can be difficult to communicate. Hand signals enable a limited vocabulary, but with the help of some simple devices we can grab attention and can even express ourselves clearly and concisely…

Underwater it can be difficult to attract the attention of others, it does not help to scream! A whistle should always be fitted to your BCD so that you can easily draw attention on the surface. But in an emergency, you can be too tired and out of breath to use it. Then it may be easier to just press a button and get a sound that is much higher than that which can be achieved with a whistle. **Air-powered signalling devices** are attached between the BCD inflator and low pressure hose. Some come with another hose and connector to the inflator because the international standard coupling doesn't provide enough air. Most models also work underwater. On the surface it should be used with caution—the sound is very loud! If this sounds a bit drastic for use underwater during a normal dive there are other options:

A **maraca** is a metal container filled with metal balls. When shaken underwater, it makes a sound that draws other divers' attentions. Also known as a shaker or rattle.

Warning: excessive use will irritate divers in the water who do not know what all the fuss is about but can still hear the noise!

A **tank banger** uses the dive cylinder (without protective net) to create a sound. A large plastic ball is held to the cylinder by a thick rubber/elastic/bungy cord. When you want to draw attention, pull out the ball and release it. Usually needs to be repeated a couple of times to achieve the intended effect.

A **reef stick** is a 50 cm/1.6 ft long metal or plastic rod that can be used to draw attention by tapping it on the dive cylinder. Many dive guides use them to point out interesting animals on the reef. Another purpose is for underwater photographers, who use this stick to stabilize themselves where it is not possible to sit on the bottom or hold on to a solid object, with minimal impact on the environment. Also, called a *muck stick* or *reef pointer*.

A **slate** can be used for notes during the dive, or to write down the dive plan — this is especially important for technical diving involving stage decompression and gas switching.

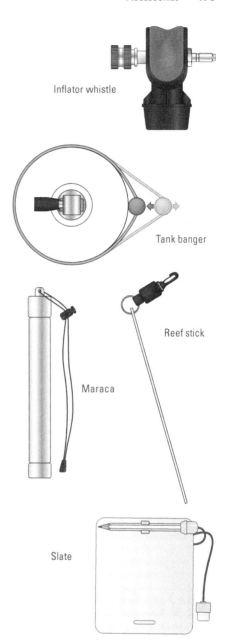

Inflator whistle

Tank banger

Reef stick

Maraca

Slate

'Save-a-Dive' Kit

There are packages you can buy in waterproof containers. However, it is easy to create your own kit that matches your equipment and the type of diving you do. If your diving is organized via a scuba diving centre, there is less need for a save-a-dive kit — they always have spare equipment because they know that things break.

However, if you dive far from assistance, you need more spare parts and contingency planning.

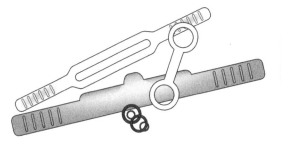

Example 'save-a-dive' kit contents: spare mask strap, fin strap, snorkel holder and O-rings for cylinder/regulators.

Hoses

Regulators, BCDs, drysuits and instruments usually come with any required hoses. But they sometimes need to be replaced.

Braided
A braided hose has three distinct layers: an inner liner of polyurethane, a middle layer of braided polyester for strength and an outer layer of braided nylon for abrasion resistance. They are lighter than rubber hoses, much more flexible and also come in many different colours.

Rubber
These are made of neoprene rubber with an internal reinforcement adjusted for the intended pressure. They have a smooth surface and excellent durability but are less flexible and come mainly in black.

Dive Bag

All this equipment must be gathered together to store and transport it. A dive bag must be durable, large enough and made of non-rotting material so it can cope with salt water. Some divers use mesh bags on boats but these are not suitable for air travel. There are even comfortable back packs with large pockets and wheels.

There are plenty to choose from. Regardless of model, a good dive bag must be large enough for the equipment you want to bring, except for weights and dive cylinder. It must also be made of a strong synthetic material to withstand wear. If there is a zipper, this should be made of a material that does not corrode. But even a plastic zipper requires maintenance—salt crystals will soon impair the function.

Traditional dive bag

As in the image. This is the simplest model. Carried by handle or a shoulder strap. Many manufacturers have completely waterproof dive bags, which is much better for your vehicle! These water-proof bags are often equipped with a drain plug, so that they can be filled with water to ease rinsing after diving. Other features may include smaller pockets for organizing.

Backpack

Just like an ordinary backpack, this facilitates carrying heavy things and frees both hands for other tasks. Backpacks often also have pockets on the sides for fins and many smaller pockets for organization of accessories.

Bag with wheels

These models are similar to soft suitcases with a retractable handle and wheels. These are best suited for transporting dry diving equipment on the road as on board a dive boat they are a bit too big and heavy.

Other bags

There are also padded smaller bags and cases for instruments and regulators, waterproof bags, plastic boxes for stuff you want to keep dry, and mesh bags mainly for mask, snorkel and fins. Drysuits are usually delivered with a special bag because it can be difficult to fit them in and it is also important to protect them from the hard stuff that you carry in your dive bag. This often also doubles as a mat to stand on whilst donning the suit.

Care and Maintenance

Always rinse your equipment in fresh water after use. Check for and prevent corrosion or ruptures in the material, and dirty or cracked O-rings. Make it a habit to regularly disassemble equipment and inspect it carefully, especially before and after prolonged intermissions in your diving. Note that all diving knives corrode (except for titanium), so cover the metal parts with a thin layer of silicone grease. It is also wise to give your dive torch some attention—an O-ring that is not sealing properly can easily lead to its destruction.

You must be careful when picking an O-ring out of its groove—a damaged sealing surface can be difficult to repair. There are special removal tools, which are similar to the small hooks dentists use, but your fingers or a credit card will work just as well. Where the O-rings are especially important, e.g. in underwater photography and diving torches, manufacturers usually include special plastic tools with their products.

With the right care and maintenance your equipment will give you reliable service for many years. It will also render a better sell-on value if you want to change or upgrade. You may find it helpful to log your services in your log book or other record. Showing that an item was properly maintained might bring a higher resale price.

CHAPTER 9

Technical Diving

Common diving apparatus is great for exploring the underwater world, at least down to 30–40 m/100–130 ft. But if you would like to go deeper or stay longer then you have to look at other ways to dive. This a brief summary to give a basic understanding of equipment-related issues.

This chapter assumes certain knowledge of decompression theory and diving physics which you will have learned in basic training.

Sport diving began in the 1950s with closed-circuit rebreathers, home-made regulators, cylinders made from old fire extinguishers and visionaries who constantly moved the limits forward. Except for refinements, better production methods and new materials, no really huge changes in the way we dive have occurred since the invention of open-circuit breathing apparatus.

There is much left to be discovered from the surface down to 30 metres, but there are many who believe that something is missing in 'recreational' diving. For those, newer techniques make diving an adventure again and we have visionaries to thank for developments. In order to take an overview of this type of diving, we have to start with a more refined definition than the common collective term 'technical diving'. The first division is the breathing gas, with a further division being the type of breathing systems used.

Breathing Gases

Common in all the gas mixtures used for diving is oxygen. We can't live without these molecules, but oxygen can also cause some problems. According to Dalton's Law, each gas in a gas mixture exerts a pressure related to the percentage of the gas. So, the partial pressure of oxygen (pO_2) in air at the surface is about 20% of the atmospheric pressure—0.2 bar.

The partial pressure of oxygen is a very important factor in all diving. It should not be too low or too high. It is dangerous if it gets lower than 0.16 bar, but in general, a pO_2 higher than 1.6 bar is considered toxic, but the length of exposure is also an important factor.

As you will already know, nitrogen is the culprit in some diving disorders. This gas functions only as a filler in the air as we don't metabolise it. However, according to Henry's Law, nitrogen is absorbed into our body in proportion to the ambient pressure. This is not a real problem in itself, but as we then decrease the pressure excess nitrogen starts to expand again. If we can't control this process as we ascend from our dives decompression sickness may be the result.

The absorbed nitrogen will also give a narcotic effect under pressure. For most divers this will occur at depths around 30–40 m/ 100–130 ft, but it varies hugely by individual. At depths beyond 50–60 m/160–200 ft, nitrogen narcosis makes it almost impossible to function at the level required to dive safely.

To reduce the problems with nitrogen we can replace nitrogen with another inert gas. As you can see in the table on page 178, all gases have advantages and disadvantages. Some of them do not cause any narcosis, even at great depths, but they are difficult to get hold of or very expensive. In addition, in the most advanced diving different gas mixtures are used for different stages of the dive. For example, normally the oxygen content is increased during ascent to help eliminate absorbed inert gases. This means that special tables must be used to plan a dive profile and the gas mixtures to be used at different depths. Starting to get complicated? Maybe, but there are computers for this purpose too.

One can imagine synthetically-manufactured gas molecules made out of other elements, but there are no such gases today that have proved useful.

Properties	Argon (Ar)	Nitrogen (N)	Neon (Ne)	Helium (He)	Hydrogen (H)
Decompression	Not usable.	Good on shorter dives, slow on longer/ deeper dives.	Rather easy to eliminate on longer dives. Accumulates slowly on short dives.	Easy to eliminate on longer dives. Accumulates rapidly on short dives.	Easy to eliminate on longer dives. Accumulates rapidly on short dives.
Narcotic potential	Very big effect.	Big effect at greater than recreational depths.	No effect.	No effect.	Some effect at very great depths (over 200 m/650 ft).
Voice distortion	Deeper voice.	None.	Almost normal voice.	Big distortion.	Big distortion.
Thermal conductivity	Good insulation.	Rather good insulation.	Rather good insulation.	Bad insulation.	Very bad insulation.
Breathing	Difficult.	Difficult at greater depths.	Rather easy.	Easy even at greater depths.	Easy even at greater depths.
Cost/ availability	Low cost, good availability.	Lowest cost, very good availability.	Very expensive depending on purity, widely available.	Relatively expensive, only available in some places.	Low cost, very good availability.

Inert gases and their potential for use as diving breathing gases.

Air

Clean, dry, filtered, compressed air is the most common breathing mixture for recreational diving. It is cheap, abundant everywhere on earth and it is quite easy to store it in your tank(s). The disadvantages are the depth limitations (around 40 m/130 ft due to the risk of nitrogen narcosis and 56 m/180 ft due to oxygen toxicity) and that the longest allowable bottom times for direct ascents to the surface sometimes feel limited.

Enriched air nitrox

One way to reduce the problem of narcosis caused by the amount of nitrogen in air is to add more oxygen. This is called nitrox, oxygen enriched air, or enriched air nitrox (shortened to EANx — x stands for the percentage of oxygen). The most common blends are 32% O_2 and 36% O_2. Another advantage is increased bottom time, but this depends (just as for air) which table we use. Some people argue that you should use nitrox with regular air tables to increase safety. This is not motivation enough for most divers for a new investment in regulator(s) and cylinders or to pay for expensive fills, and if we accept this reasoning we must therefore consider air diving as not safe.

The big disadvantage with oxygen enriched air is that the deepest allowable depth is always less than for air. The partial pressure of oxygen sets the limit. To work out the max depth you must first decide how high a pO_2 can be tolerated and for how long. Most educational organizations set max pO_2 to 1.6 bar (for decompression) but many governing bodies advocate 1.4 bar during the main part of the dive—follow your training.

Heliox

Helium is the gas with the least narcotic effect, so it seems obvious that it is a good replacement for nitrogen in the breathing mixture. Unfortunately, helium causes a neurological and physiological diving disorder called 'High Pressure Nervous Syndrome' (HPNS). This can occur below depths of about 140 m/460 ft, and common signs are seizures, tremors and personality changes.

Helium vents faster than nitrogen during ascent, so normally the first decompression stop must be made deeper compared with nitrogen-based gas mixtures. By replacing nitrogen with helium in the breathing gas, you eliminate narcosis and breathing is facilitated as helium has lower density. However, heliox is a relatively expensive gas mixture, especially for open breathing systems.

Hydrox

This is a mixture of hydrogen and oxygen, which is rarely used by scuba divers. Hydrogen is a very accessible gas with no significant narcotic effect. The main drawback is the risk of explosion if it is mixed with more than 4% oxygen. It requires several stages of other breathing mix for shallower depths before switching to hydrox.

Experiments have shown that hydrox can be used for very deep diving (500–700 m/1600–2300 ft) but the procedures for the transition between gas mixtures used at shallower depths and hydrox must be well planned. It is also important to take into account the risk of hydrogen narcosis—the same type of effect as nitrogen narcosis but of a more hallucinatory nature (nitrogen narcosis is more like alcohol intoxication).

Trimix

Most mixed-gas diving is made using trimix. This gas blend combines the low narcotic effect of helium, the lower need to decompress nitrogen, the elimination of the risk of HPNS and a lower cost than for heliox. Divers decide the balance between cost, time for decompression and the degree of narcotic effect to determine the fractions of helium and nitrogen. Just as with heliox diving, decompression is usually made with some nitrox blend or even pure oxygen (max depth 6 m/20 ft).

With all deep diving, you must consider oxygen toxicity and narcosis. With trimix it is possible to control both these factors. The first experiments with trimix were an attempt to avoid the problems with HPNS, but it was soon realized that trimix had several other benefits. Trimix is now used among recreational divers by those who want to dive deeper than is considered safe with air and nitrox (generally 40 m/130 ft), but also by scuba divers who want to be able to think clearly in shallower depths, for example underwater photographers.

When you choose your blend, you must consider several factors: degree of narcosis that is acceptable; time for decompression; acceptable pO_2 during the dive; type of diving equipment; safety margin; and surface support. A common trimix blend for 40 m/130 ft is 45% N_2, 30% He and 25% O_2. For greater depths the percentage of oxygen is reduced and the percentage of helium is increased. During the ascent one or two switches of breathing mix are usually made to reduce the time for decompression.

Technical Diving Equipment

The major disadvantage of an open-circuit system is the waste of breathing gas. Of the gas we draw into our lungs with every breath, only a small fraction is used. The rest is released into the water. In order to dive longer and deeper than conventional air tables permit we have two challenges: gas supply and gas blend.

Typical set-up

Standard diving apparatus for technical diving is a twinset consisting of two 12 litre/80 cu ft cylinders (usually steel for their weight in water) connected by a manifold with an isolating valve.

1. Twin tank

The most common set up for technical diving with a drysuit is two 12 litre, 232 bar steel cylinders. In warmer water 80 cu ft aluminium cylinders can be used. The cylinders are connected by a manifold with an isolating valve. For some dives, this gas supply must be supplemented with both more bottom gas and decompression gas, so a critical part of the dive plan is calculating gas consumption.

2. Wing BCD

As in technical diving you carry a large amount of equipment, it is important that the BCD is capable of lifting all this weight. Lifting capacity should be around 20 kg/45 lbs. Many manufacturers have wings in different sizes so you can adapt the BCD to your diving. For technical diving in a drysuit heavier stainless steel back plates are preferable Some training

stipulates that the harness should not have any quick release buckles, as they are seen as a point of failure. You will need enough D-rings to attach all your accessories.

3. Primary second stage

The regulators must be good quality and high performance. Both regulators should be of the same brand and model so that you do not need to carry different spare parts.

The primary second stage is often connected using a long hose (210 cm/7 ft) to the right-hand first stage. The hose is routed down behind the wing, up across the chest and around the neck. It should have a trigger hook so that it can be attached to the harness when it is not in use. The reason for the extra length is that — if trained and practised — you donate your primary second stage in the event of gas sharing.

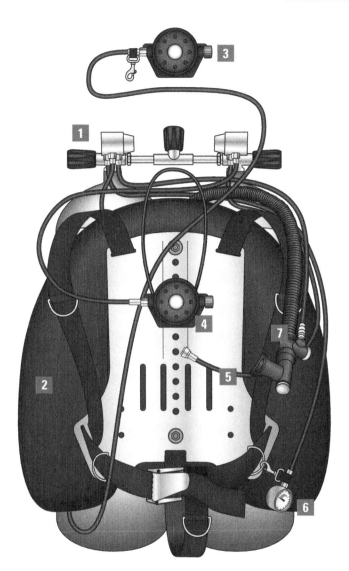

This contrasts with normal recreational diving where you usually have an alternate second stage with only a slightly longer hose than you have on your primary regulator.

4. Extra second stage

The extra second stage is connected to the left first stage with a full-length hose. The hose is routed behind the neck so that it comes in from the right-hand side. It is held close to you with a rubber holder (or 'necklace') worn around the neck.

5. Inflator hose for drysuit

If you dive with a drysuit, you normally attach the hose to the left first stage and the hose is routed under your left arm. If you dive with helium mixes, a separate suit gas cylinder is used.

6. Pressure gauge

The submersible pressure gauge is normally fixed to the left first stage and attached with a trigger hook to a D-ring on the left side of the harness. It is important that it is built for deep dives. Otherwise the increased external pressure deforms the housing, this can interfere with the internal mechanism.

7. Inflator

An inflator with large metal parts in the mechanism facilitates service, is less sensitive to interference, and can be easily serviced in the field (and even underwater). The corrugated hose attaches to the wing behind the neck so that it does not interfere with hose routing from the two first stages.

This is just the basic set up that often needs to be supplemented with cylinders of extra bottom gas and decompression gas depending on the dive profile, and suit gas if trimix is used. These extra cylinders are usually aluminium because they are close to neutral in water or positive, and when used they can be sent to the surface.

You must have a system for attaching the extra cylinders to your wing harness. Cylinder handling during the dive is a skill you should practice and part of dive planning. This type of diving requires education and training, a fairly substantial investment in equipment and appropriate surface support.

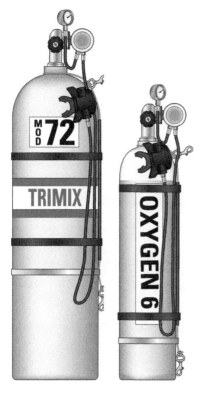

Extra bottom gas

A standard 2×12 litre twinset contains up to approximately 5500 litres gas, which might not be sufficient for some deep and long dives. You could use a larger twinset, or extra side-slung cylinders with bottom gas. Extra cylinders for bottom gas are often made of aluminium (11 litres/80 cu ft) for near neutral buoyancy.

These cylinders are usually rigged to hang to one side or the other—'side slung'—using two stainless steel trigger hooks on nylon cords/straps, one just below the neck and one towards the bottom of the cylinder so that it will sit in a good position in the water when it is attached to the harness D-rings. You can buy kits for different size cylinders.

The cylinders **must be clearly marked with the MOD** (maximum operating depth) of the gas they contain to help avoid misuse.

Decompression gas

During ascent, gas mixtures with high percentage of oxygen are used for faster release of the inert gas. This could be trimix for deep dives, with pure oxygen from 6 m/20 ft. Otherwise, EAN50 is common as decompression gas.

The cylinders **must be clearly marked with the MOD** (maximum operating depth) of the gas they contain to help avoid misuse.

Generally, divers use aluminium cylinders for decompression gas because of their near neutral buoyancy. Standard sizes are 5.5 litres (40 cu ft) or 7 litres (50 cu ft).

Drysuit gas

If you dive in a drysuit and breathe helium mixes, because of its poor thermal properties you will need a separate suit cylinder with argon (or air) to reduce cooling. The capacity of the suit cylinder is normally around 1.5 litres (8 cu ft).

As this first stage is not connected to a second stage, it is important that it has a pressure relief valve in order to avoid damage in the case of malfunction.

The location of the suit cylinder depends on your personal configuration, but it is usually attached to the back plate with straps.

Sidemount

When it comes to balance in the water, it does not really make sense to have the heaviest part of your scuba gear on your back. When diving with a sidemount rig, all cylinders are attached to your sides — balance is not only better, you are also more streamlined. Sidemount diving began as a specialized technique for advanced cave diving, where the position of the cylinders — plus the ability to detach them — made it easier to get through tight spaces. These advantages also apply to wreck penetration and diving in other confined spaces.

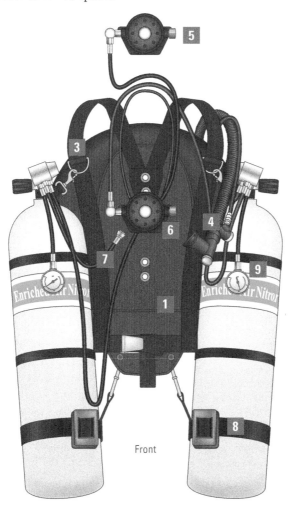

Front

1. Sidemount BCD

Sidemount diving requires either a standard wing or a bladder specially adapted for this type of diving. It looks more like a backpack and sits in the centre of your back. The harness/back plate has a so-called 'buttplate' at the bottom where the lower trigger hooks are attached. You can find separate buttplates to be installed on a normal back plate, but also BCDs dedicated to sidemount diving.

2. Lower attachment

The lower trigger hook on the cylinder is connected to rings on the 'buttplate'. The length of the cord (nylon or rubber) between the cylinder and trigger hook should be adapted for good balance in the water.

3. Upper attachment

The upper trigger hook on the cylinder is connected to the upper D-ring on your BCD harness.

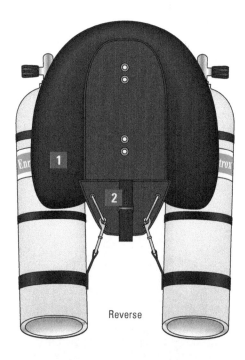

Reverse

4. Inflator

There are some different opinions on how the inflator and the corrugated hose should best be placed. The illustration shows a traditional wing and location of the inflator. On some specially developed sidemount wings, the corrugated hose is attached at the left hip.

5. Right second stage

As with a twinset, the regulators must be of good quality and have good performance. The two regulators should be of the same brand and model so that you don't need to carry different spares.

The right-hand second stage is connected with a long hose (210 cm/7 ft) to the right-hand first stage. The hose is routed down toward the right hip, up across the chest and around the neck.

The hose is often connected with an elbow fitting to the second stage, either fixed or swivel to enable a comfortable and streamlined hose routing. These often come with a set of sidemount-specific regulators but can bought separately.

It is this second stage you donate if you need to share your breathing gas.

6. Left second stage

The left second stage has a shorter hose than the right. The hose is routed behind the neck so that it comes in from the right-hand side. The second stage is held close to you with a rubber cord (necklace) around the neck. Like the right-hand second stage this often has an elbow fitting, either fixed or swivel to get the correct routing of the hose.

7. Inflator hose for drysuit

This hose is placed on the right-hand first stage.

8. Weights

Often placed on lower part of the cylinders to improve balance in the water.

9. Pressure gauge

The pressure gauge is mounted on a short hose so as to be easy to check.

Sidemount also has advantages in general decompression diving. As before, you attach as many cylinders as you need to conduct the dive. But unlike twinset diving, with a sidemount configuration you can see and adjust[1] all of your valves and regulators and can more easily deal with any problems.

---

1   Twinset divers are trained to perform 'shutdowns'—reaching behind to turn off the pillar valves if there is a problem with a first stage. However, this involves technique, practice and flexibility which some divers simply do not have.

It is possible to sidemount dive with just one cylinder, but balance in the water is better with two or more. This style of diving therefore has limited relevance for normal recreational diving. But for longer dives with nitrox, sidemount gives all the above advantages for a limited additional investment.

Rebreathers

The first working oxygen rebreathers were designed in the early twentieth century, and during the Second World War they were used on sabotage missions. Later, there was a new era of development with applications in the space race, as closed systems were needed for space walks.

In the 1980s, more divers began to investigate the possibilities of diving deeper and longer. It was not difficult to identify the disadvantages with open systems for this kind of diving, and closed systems were only manufactured for military use. Manufacturers saw no private market for these units, so the price remained high. There was also a fear that the new inventions might fall into the hands of enemies. So it was left to a small group of enthusiasts, mainly in the USA, to experiment with closed systems and there are now several brands on the market, even if at the time of writing prices are still a deterrent for most recreational divers. But with closed systems we are not talking about science fiction, they exist and they work very well. Modern computer technology has improved the monitoring of important parameters, so systems are more advanced than ever.

One of the major challenges is the removal of carbon dioxide (CO_2) from exhaled gas in an efficient and safe manner. The idea used by rebreathers is to bond the CO_2 gas chemically with a solid substance in a 'scrubber' (see page 188) and then it also loses most of its volume. Several compounds have been used for the CO_2-scrubber, but at low temperatures all of them have decreased efficiency, and they all cause a strong reaction with water. So it is important for designers to make sure that the water that enters the breathing loop cannot reach the CO_2-scrubber.

A major difference between closed and open-circuit systems is that with a closed system you breathe from a flexible bag called a 'counterlung'. If you tried to take a breath from a wine bottle you would understand why—you can't breathe from a rigid container. Breathing via this bag means that you keep a constant volume of gas, and your buoyancy does not change with your breathing.

The greatest users of rebreathers are still the military, but they have many advantages for recreational divers. One is that they are much quieter in the water than open systems as they release few bubbles. This makes it easier to get close to wildlife, which is appreciated by most of us but especially photographers. Other benefits include: using less breathing gas during a dive; the gas is not as dry as in open systems; and we do not need to warm the air as we breath, thus conserving energy and heat. There are more benefits and these are detailed in the rest of this chapter as we look at the two different types of rebreather.

Continued development, greater volume of sales and reducing production costs due to economies of scale make it reasonable to believe that rebreathers will become more and more common amongst recreational divers.

Semi-closed-circuit rebreather (SCR)

In a semi-closed system there is no separate oxygen cylinder, you do the dive with a breathing gas of a predetermined enhanced oxygen fraction. The gas flows to the counterlung at a pre-set rate to replace the consumed oxygen. There are also models with a computer that controls this and on many models it is possible to manually add gas if needed. Since gas flows continuously to the counterlung, excess gas will seep out through its pressure relief valve. Gas will also be released during ascent.

Advantages of semi-closed systems:
- Lower gas consumption than open systems.
- Breathing gas circulates, so it is warmer and less dry than with open-circuit.
- Standard regulator can be used in the event of an emergency.
- Often easier to obtain nitrox than pure oxygen (needed for CCR—page 188).

Disadvantages/problems with semi-closed systems:
- Require more care and maintenance before and after dives than open-circuit.
- More expensive than open-circuit.
- Require in-depth training.
- Buoyant in the water, need more lead when diving in colder water compared to a SCUBA twinset.
- Gas partial pressure varies with depth, unlike CCR (see page 188).

1. Mouthpiece
The mouthpiece has two check valves to control gas flow. It also has a shut-off valve to prevent water entering the system when the mouthpiece is not in place in the mouth. Some models also have LEDs to show if everything is working properly, or if there is a problem. There are also mouthpieces with a built-in open system that can be used in the case of malfunction of the semi-closed system.

2. Open second stage regulator
In the case of malfunction of the semi-closed system, a standard second stage can be used to abort the dive.

3. First stage
The first stage regulator is basically the same as a standard scuba regulator but adapted for the breathing gas used—for concentrations of oxygen higher than 40% it will need to be fitted with the correct seals and O-rings.

4. Nitrox cylinder
This is an aluminium or steel cylinder approximately 4–5 litres/28–35 cu ft. Dives with semi-closed systems are almost exclusively made with nitrox blends between 32 and 60% oxygen. Since the gas in the cylinder is used to replace the oxygen consumed by breathing, it would be fairly pointless having air in the cylinder.

5. Flow limiter
The flow limiter controls how much new gas is added per minute. In a purely mechanical device this is pre-set for different nitrox blends—the higher the oxygen fraction in the breathing gas the less the flow. There are also semi-closed systems with an oxygen sensor and electronics that control the addition of new breathing gas.

6. Pressure gauge
This is a standard submersible pressure gauge for keeping an eye on the gas supply.

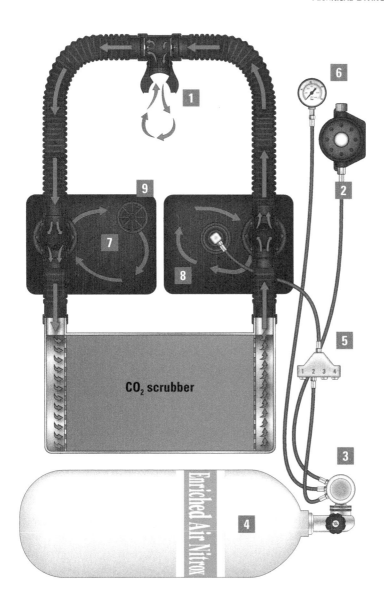

CO₂ scrubber

Enriched Air Nitrox

7. Counterlung — exhalation

The counterlung must be flexible to maintain constant volume during the respiratory cycle. As the circulated gas volume is constant, buoyancy does not change with respiration. The counterlung also captures some of the water vapour in the exhaled gas, most of it condenses into water in the bag.

The connection between the hose and counterlung has valves to direct the gas flow. See the arrows in the illustration.

8. Counterlung — inhalation

This is much like the counterlung for exhalation except that addition of breathing gas is made to this bag via a hose from the flow limiter. Connections can also be made for manual filling and a demand valve that adds gas when you inhale deeply.

9. Pressure relief valve

Because of the constant addition of new gas, there is a pressure relief valve in the exhalation counterlung to release the surplus. Gas will also be vented through this valve during the ascent.

CO2 scrubber

This has the task of removing the carbon dioxide from the exhaled air through a chemical reaction that forms a solid compound. As you can see in the table below, only a small part of the oxygen in each breath is metabolised—most remains in the exhaled gas. But the carbon dioxide must be removed before the gas can be re-breathed.

Amount in air	Inhaled air (%)	Expired air (%)	Cause
Oxygen	21	16	Oxygen transferred from air to blood
Carbon dioxide (CO_2)	0.03	4	Carbon dioxide transferred from blood
Nitrogen	78	78	Nitrogen is not used by the body
Water vapour	Varied	Varied, but more than inhaled air	Water evaporates from the mucous membranes in the airways

The carbon dioxide in a gas can be removed in different ways. Intensive on-going research is trying to find a solution to the increasing amount of carbon dioxide in our atmosphere. The technology scientists develop may in the future be used to increase the efficiency of our CO_2 scrubbers... until then, they are based on granular soda lime, which consists of calcium hydroxide with a small amount of sodium hydroxide as a catalyst.

The overall reaction is:

$$CO_{2(g)}+Ca(OH)_{2(s)} \rightarrow CaCO_{3(s)}+H_2O_{(l)}$$

For the process to start, a small amount of water is needed. However, too much water can cause a violent reaction. The breathing circuit and the scrubber must have a means to remove some of the water vapour formed by breathing. In most devices, the diver has to pack the soda lime into the scrubber, but you can also buy it in cartridges that give a diving time of approximately three hours.

Closed-circuit rebreather (CCR)

A closed system has at least two separate cylinders, one with oxygen and one with diluent gas. The diluent can be air, nitrox or trimix depending on the purpose of the dive and planned dive profile. You are totally dependent on the electronics to control the composition of your breathing gas. So for added safety there are usually two or more fully independent computer systems. The electronics also monitor your dive profile and computer displays important data.

Advantages of closed systems:
- Consumption of breathing gas depends only on body metabolism, depth does not affect it.
- Computer-controlled system blends the optimal gas mix for every depth reached during the dive, maintaining constant partial pressure of oxygen (pO_2).
- Makes it possible to dive deep and long.
- As the gas is circulated, it is warmer and less dry compared with open systems.
- Cheaper gas bills than open-circuit for diving similar depths/times, as far less is consumed.

Disadvantages/problems with closed systems:

- Need a lot of care and maintenance before and after dives.
- Expensive to buy, at least at the time of writing.
- Need special education and training to use.
- Buoyant in the water, need more lead than open-circuit.
- Totally computer dependant.
- Usually, a completely independent bailout/alternate source is also required.

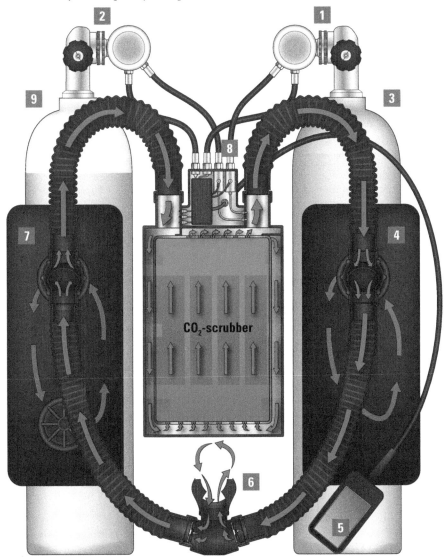

1. Regulator — diluent
The first stage for the diluent is a standard scuba regulator adapted for the breathing gas used. Some closed systems have an open system second stage integrated in the mouthpiece in case of malfunction. Connected with a standard low-pressure hose from the first stage to the diluent. There may also be a separate second stage for use as a bailout. It can only be used if the gas is safe at the problem depth.

2. Regulator — oxygen
The first stage on the oxygen cylinder must be completely compatible with 100% oxygen.

3. Diluent

The diluent gas can be plain air, nitrox or trimix depending on the purpose of the dive and dive profile. Even a closed system consumes *some* gas for purposes other than breathing during a dive, i.e. filling a drysuit and depth variations.

4. Counterlung — inhalation

The counterlung must be flexible so as to obtain a constant volume between it and the lungs during the respiratory cycle. Since the circulated gas volume is constant, buoyancy does not change with respiration. The counterlung also has to capture some of the water vapour in the exhaled gas, most of which is condensed into water in the breathing loop.

The connection between the hose and the counterlung has flanges to direct the gas flow in to or out of the counterlung.

The addition of breathing gas is made to this bag via a hose from the diluent first stage. Connections can also be made for manual addition of diluent gas, for example, to adjust the buoyancy.

5. Computer display

Shows important data for the dive and is used to set default values for important dive parameters, for example, pO_2 and type of diluent.

6. Mouthpiece

The mouthpiece has two check valves to control gas flow. It also has a shut-off valve to prevent water entering the system when the mouthpiece is not in place in the mouth. Some models also have LEDs to show if everything is working properly, or if there is a problem. There are also mouthpieces with a built-in

open system that can be used in the case of malfunction of the closed system.

7. Counterlung — exhalation

This counterlung normally has a pressure relief valve to release gas excess.

8. CO_2 scrubber

This has to remove the carbon dioxide from the exhaled air through a chemical reaction that forms a solid compound, just like in the semi-closed rebreather (see page 188).

9. Oxygen

This is an aluminium or steel cylinder with a capacity of 2 or 3 litres/14 or 21 cu ft. The oxygen consumed during metabolism is replaced. Normal oxygen consumption, regardless of depth, is usually around 1–1.5 litres/0.035–0.053 cu ft per minute.

10. Computer

The computer is both the closed system's brain and central controlling unit. Oxygen partial pressure is measured by several independent sensors (2 or 3). The result is analysed by the computer and compared with the set value for pO_2. If it deviates, a signal is sent to one of the relays that control the valves for oxygen or diluent, opening them to balance the gas mixture.

High-pressure hoses from the two first stages are also connected to the computer so that tank pressure can be monitored.

The central electronic unit is also a dive computer whose display (usually wrist-mounted) shows important dive data. Post-dive, modern systems can use wireless methods (e.g. Bluetooth) to send information to a personal computer (PC) or to connect to the manufacturer's server to analyse any problems.

Oxygen sensors do not measure percentage of gas, but partial pressure. Normally you set the desired partial pressure of oxygen, which is then constant during the entire dive. This means that the percentage of oxygen varies with depth.

The table (on page 191) shows values for different depths for both open and closed systems. The closed system is set for a pO_2 of 1.3 bar, but this may be adjusted higher or lower depending on the dive profile and safety margin. The table shows the major benefits of a closed system regarding the uptake of nitrogen — the percentage of nitrogen is significantly lower in the breathing gas compared with diving on a open system, at least until a depth of 50 m/165 ft.

However, below 40 m / 130 ft it is sensible to use trimix to replace some of the nitrogen and reduce the effects of narcosis (see page 179). You use trimix instead of nitrox as diluent gas, choosing a suitable blend for the planned depth. For dives down to about 50 metres the trimix blend can have the same percentage (normoxic) or more oxygen (hyperoxic) than air. For deeper dives the mix must start to have less oxygen than air (hypoxic), but the specifics are beyond the scope of this book and should be learned on course.

Depth m (ft)	Pressure bar	Open system				Closed system			
		pO$_2$ bar	O$_2$ %	pN$_2$ bar	N$_2$ %	pO$_2$ bar	O$_2$ %	pN$_2$ bar	N$_2$ %
3 (10)	1.3	0.27	21	1.03	79	1.3	100	0	0
6 (20)	1.6	0.34	21	1.26	79	1.3	81	0.3	19
10 (33)	2.0	0.42	21	1.58	79	1.3	65	0.7	35
15 (50)	2.5	0.52	21	1.98	79	1.3	52	1.2	48
20 (66)	3.0	0.63	21	2.37	79	1.3	43	1.7	57
30 (100)	4.0	0.84	21	3.16	79	1.3	32	2.7	68
40 (130)	5.0	1.05	21	3.95	79	1.3	26	3.7	74
50 (160)	6.0	1.26	21	4.74	79	1.3	21	4.7	79

Comparison of open and closed systems — partial pressures of breathing gases at different depths.

Summary

From the survey of breathing mixtures, we can see that air is easy and cheap to use but has some limitations for deep diving. If you are prepared to take up the challenge of technical training, acquiring new and extending existing diving equipment, having more complex dive preparations, dive planning and implementation, there being potential for more to go wrong and higher costs, then there are great opportunities with this type of diving. You can, for example, dive on wrecks which are not accessible with conventional scuba kit and there is completely different wildlife at greater depths.

Care and Maintenance

Most technical diving gear requires the same attention as its counterparts for recreational diving — wash thoroughly in fresh water, dry and store in a cool place out of the sun. Rebreathers need a bit more care. Before diving you must pack the scrubber canister with carbon dioxide-absorbent granulates. If you are not diving again for some days, you need to take the rebreather apart and rinse it carefully. The breathing loop must be disinfected and dried, since the warm and moist environment is perfect for growing micro-organisms. The used absorbent must be discarded and the canister rinsed and dried. Because the type of diving being done is generally more serious it is vitally important to thoroughly check over kit before and after each use.

CHAPTER 10

Speculating on the Future

'The future is here – it's just not very evenly distributed'.

If we are to believe the author William Gibson and the quote above, the future is electronically controlled closed-circuit rebreathers. They already exist and they work extremely well, but they are still nowhere near as common as open-circuit. Greater availability and, above all, a lower price, will perhaps enable these advanced diving apparatuses to fully out-compete the open system. But there are many who argue that the open system is so simple, safe and cheap that it will continue to dominate for a long time to come.

The development potential of open-circuit would appear to be fairly limited, so possible progress is likely to be in better manufacturing techniques and new materials—not the operating principle of the open system as such.

The Future is Not Google-able

This is also a quote from William Gibson. It is always impossible to predict the future—the only thing we can safely say is that it will not be as it is now. Despite the rather limited chance of being correct there are many who devote their waking time to trying to figure out what our society will look like in 25, 50 or 100 years time. But the only common denominator is that most are likely be proved wrong. So we conclude by giving a short summary of some research areas and a little speculation about the future. The three areas, which are most promising for the future of diving are chemical decompression, liquid breathing and artificial gills.

Chemical Decompression

The idea is that the absorbed inert gas (nitrogen or helium) should be eliminated in a method other than through the lungs. Researchers are trying to find an enzyme that can transform a gas into a chemical compound that can be released from the body in our urine. There are many problems to be solved, but chief amongst them is finding an enzyme that can both do the job and be accepted by our immune system.

If this research continues, maybe one day we will take a pill instead of doing decompression stops after a long and/or deep dive.[1]

---

1   Based on notes from a lecture by Professor Hans Örnhagen, www.ornhagen.se See also news. bbc.co.uk/1/hi/health/3563679.stm and www.ncbi.nlm.nih.gov/pubmed/14724207

Liquid Breathing

With an incompressible liquid in the lungs, it is much easier to control the contents than with a gas. Therefore, with liquid breathing we would be able to dive without getting any inert gas in our body at all, and thus have no time limit.

The problem is finding a liquid that can dissolve enough oxygen in gas form and that has no destructive effect on the delicate lung tissue. Since a liquid has considerably higher density than a gas, we also need some mechanism that circulates the liquid, especially during hard work, to provide enough oxygen for our metabolism.

This may sound like science fiction, but research with animals as big as goats and dogs has looked promising. In the most extreme experiments, mice have been pressurised down to 1000 metres followed by a direct ascent to atmospheric pressure. No abnormal behaviour could be detected.[2]

Artificial Gills

Many aquatic animals have the ability to use the oxygen that is dissolved in water. Common to all of them, from single-celled organisms to fish, is a very low metabolism, so the small amount of oxygen in the water is enough—even for fast swimmers like tuna. The higher animals that live in water, such as sea turtles and whales, have evolved from terrestrial animals and must surface to breathe—there are no animals in these groups with gills.

As mammals, our tissues have a rather big demand for oxygen, especially during exercise, so we can't compare ourselves with fish in this respect. Even if it were possible to make artificial gills with the same efficiency as fish gills, we would have to move like a torpedo underwater to get sufficient oxygen for our needs. Another disappointing fact is that the warmer the water is, the less oxygen it can hold.

It is possible that in the future scientists will find chemical compounds that attract oxygen better than haemoglobin, but at present this possibility doesn't look too promising.

---

2   Again see Professor Hans Örnhagen, www.ornhagen.se and also www.independent.co.uk/news/science/into-the-abyss-the-diving-suit-that-turns-men-into-fish-2139167.html

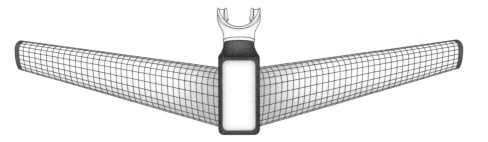

The illustration is a vision of how a future diving apparatus could look, based on a not-yet-invented technology designed to extract enough oxygen from the water to meet our needs. Some consider it really appealing — a mouthpiece, a central unit and 'gills' on each side!

Conclusion

It is difficult to speculate with complete confidence about how we will dive in 20 or 50 years' time — the only thing that is certain is that research goes on and that we will constantly get new materials and methods for our activity. The articles referenced here are from some years ago. With the rapid development of remotely-operated underwater robots it is most probably hard to find funds for research on hyperbaric physiology. So it may have to wait…

However, it is safe to assume that the type of diving we are accustomed to for our explorations under the surface will exist for a long time from now. Open circuit diving apparatus is so simple that it is likely to be the first choice for most divers for many years to come.

Index

For log books visit DivedUp.com

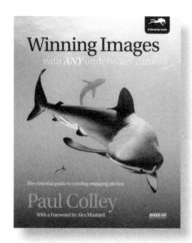

Lightning Source UK Ltd.
Milton Keynes UK
UKOW07f1343240616

276997UK00003B/13/P